A BIRD'S-EYE VIEW OF PICTURESQUE INDIA

A BIRD'S-EYE VIEW OF PICTURESQUE INDIA

BY

SIR RICHARD TEMPLE, BART.,

G.C.S.I., D.C.L. (OXON), LL.D. (CANTAB), F.R.S.

GYAN

Published by

Gyan Publishing House
5, Ansari Road
Daryaganj, New Delhi-110002
Phone: 011-47034999, 9811692060
E-mail: books@gyanbooks.com

Distribution Network
gyanbooks.com
India, USA, Canada, UK, Australia

ISBN: 978-93-6208-527-6 (HB)

First Published, 1898

2nd Impression 2024

Printed at: Gyan Press, Delhi.

A BIRD'S-EYE VIEW OF PICTURESQUE INDIA

Author: RICHARD TEMPLE

A BIRD'S-EYE VIEW OF PICTURESQUE INDIA

RIVER INDUS AT ATTOK

A BIRD'S-EYE VIEW OF PICTURESQUE INDIA

BY

THE RIGHT HONOURABLE

SIR RICHARD TEMPLE, BART., G.C.S.I.,

D.C.L. (OXON.), LL.D. (CANTAB.), F.R.S.

SOMETIME FINANCE MINISTER OF INDIA,
LIEUTENANT-GOVERNOR OF BENGAL, GOVERNOR OF BOMBAY

WITH THIRTY-TWO ILLUSTRATIONS

LONDON

CHATTO & WINDUS

1898

PREFACE

THE greater part of this work was originally written in the shape of articles for the Syndicate of Northern Newspapers at Kendal. These articles accordingly appeared in many newspapers during the early months of this year 1898, under the general title of "Picturesque India." It has now been determined to republish them together in a book, with some important additions and improvements, each article making a Chapter of the work in its new form. The scheme was, and still is, to present "a Bird's-eye View of Picturesque India," which is the title adopted for the book. Such a purview naturally embraced the principal features in the India of to-day, the land, the people, and the government. But, to render this more complete than it would otherwise have been, three new Chapters have been added—namely, "III. A Summer's Sojourn in the Himalaya"; "XI. Historic Remains and Ruins"; "XII., Episodes in History and their Localities." Thus the work at first consisted of nine Chapters; it now consists of twelve; and to these nine Chapters some improvements have been added. Further, a new feature has been introduced, the introduction of which was not possible in the original work—namely, that of illustration in black and white. For such illustration I happen to possess abundant materials, having been all my life a diligent sketcher in water-colour, and of later years in oil also. From my portfolios, containing literally hundreds of pictures, there have been selected thirty subjects specially suited to illustrate the text of the several Chapters. These pictures have been reproduced by a photographic process, so that they exactly represent at least the outlines and the shades of the pictures.

PREFACE

Although the necessary limitations of such a book as this, on so enormous a subject as India, must be evident, still, it may be well to remind the general reader of what is, and what is not, to be expected from a work like this. Though not, as I hope, unlearned, yet it does not presume to address itself to the world of Oriental learning. Though not uninformed as to the method and the results of our rule in India, it does not undertake to supply information regarding the legislation, the administration, the land tenures, the trade and industry of a vast and varied Empire. Though it gives here and there the sum total of figures which, from their magnitude, deserve recollection and can easily be remembered, it presents no statistics properly so called. Though describing the ideas, the temper, and spirit of the Natives, it does not attempt any account of their customs, inasmuch as such an account would have to enter into the lives of the various classes in many nationalities. Though touching lightly on the historic eras and epochs which have preceded, or led up to, the present British era, it hardly essays even a synopsis of the antiquities and the mediæval history of the Indian continent and peninsula. Though routes and places are freely mentioned, yet the work is not at all a handbook in the technical sense of the term.

The real object of the work, then, is in this wise. There is a growing sense among British people regarding the absolute importance of the Indian Empire to the well-being of the British Isles. Consequently there must be an increasing number of persons who wish to acquire some knowledge which, though not profound nor adequate, is far from being superficial and is not wholly insufficient—who have an idea that the country must be picturesque, and desire to have some more definite notion as to what the beauties are. More especially the number increases of travellers who are unable, indeed, to undertake extensive travel, but who will make a comprehensive tour of six months, or at the most of a year. The benefit and pleasure to be derived from such tours are manifest to all thoughtful and cultured people. The enlightenment too is remarkable, provided always that the traveller be not tempted to pronounce offhand on questions which can hardly be determined except by long service or residence in the country. Such travellers would need at the outset some general explanation regarding the whole Empire, which would be in some degree sufficient, should they have no time for enlarged reading, and would help them to pursue any particular subject whenever they might require some study of details in other books. It is for persons of both these important classes that this work is intended.

For the names of places I have adhered to the old spelling in all cases where the word has been used for history in an English form—and most of the names in this book belong to that class. In other cases the more scientific spelling known as Hunterian has been adopted.

The book begins with an Introduction,

Chapter I., setting forth the condition of India in the year 1897–8. That year happened to be one of misfortunes, for most of which a termination has been vouchsafed by Providence. The reader, so to speak, breaks ground in India itself by Chapter II. "A Winter's Tour in India," and by Chapter III. "A Summer's Sojourn in the Himalaya." These projects of comprehensive travel are followed by Chapter IV. on "The Forests and Wild Sports of India," which things may or may not be connected with travel according to the disposition of the traveller. The Land having thus been touched upon, a brief description is given of the People, with their nationalities and religions, of the Native Princes with their Courts and camps, in Chapters V., VI., and VII. The Land and the People having thus been noticed, it is time to refer to the governance and administration of the country. As a preliminary to this, some account is presented of "The Frontiers of India," in Chapter VIII., especially those on the north-west and the south-east. On this there follow Chapter IX. with the title "How India is Governed"; and Chapter X. "Progress of India under British Rule." These ten chapters, then, comprise the essential substance of the work according to its original design. But perhaps a traveller or a student, who had proceeded so far and noticed so much as is assumed to have been the case, would desire to understand the broad outlines of the history and the antiquities, of all which he will have observed many traces, but which are too vast and complex for him to study with any minuteness. Therefore Chapters XI. and XII. have been added, on "Historic Remains and Ruins," and on "Episodes in History and their Localities."

Although no statistics are embodied in the Chapters, still some readers might like to refresh their memory by an easy reference to leading facts, therefore in an Appendix are presented three tables: first, that of the principal figures relating to India; the second, that of the dates of the principal epochs in her history; third, that of the Governors-

General and Viceroys. A compact map of India, kindly lent by the proprietors of "Whitaker's Almanack," is prefixed to the work.

Most of the facts mentioned in this work are the results of British heroism and endurance, yet there is no space for attempting any record of the heroes themselves, military, civil, political.

The aim throughout has been to render the exposition easy and popular. The subject, though interesting, is alien to British thoughts; though demanding a comprehensive treatment, it is yet, in many respects, highly technical. The difficulties are great in rendering it, on the one hand, easily intelligible to the ordinary English reader; and yet, on the other hand, technically accurate. I have tried to overcome these difficulties so far as may be possible. Moreover, many of the things as here set forth are, after all, matters of judgment and opinion, sometimes also of controversy. Many a page in this book contains allusions which might give rise to objections that could not be met without an explanation for which there is no space. So also, again, many a general consideration verges on details which might, from some points of view, be deemed essential, but for which, again, space could not be found; and consequently some sense of unavoidable incompleteness might arise. For all that is stated, however, there is my own cognisance, practice, study, and observation. He who shall master all that is written in this very limited work will know the substance of much that is best worth knowing, so far, at least, as my own knowledge goes after long experience.

It may be well here to give some descriptive list of the illustrations. The number being limited to thirty-two, they have been distributed so as best to suit the tenour of each Chapter. The first Chapter, being introductory, has no illustration. The second Chapter, "A Winter's Tour in India," is illustrated (1) by a distant prospect of the promontories, the islands, and the harbour of Bombay; (2) by a view of the famous Taj Mehal, the gem of all India, as seen in the middle distance from the fortress of Agra —indeed, from the balcony where the dying Emperor Shah Jehan was placed to direct his last looks at the matchless mausoleum which he had erected; by views from (3) the citadel of Lahore, with the Mogul mosque and the tomb of Ranjit Sing, the Lion King of the Sikh nationality; and of the (4—used as Frontispiece to this volume) crossing of the Indus at Attok in the days before the great river was spanned by a railway viaduct, and as it must have looked when Alexander the Great crossed it; and (5) by a picture of the beautiful Eden Gardens on the bank of the Hooghly near Calcutta; next (6) by a picture of the carved teakwood vestibule of the temple at Nagpore, in the centre of India, being one of the few surviving examples of the woodwork for which the Mahrattas were once celebrated; and lastly, (7) by an outline of the rock of Trichinopoly, around which were waged some of the contests between the English and the French for the possession of Southern India.

The third Chapter, "A Summer's Sojourn in the Himalaya," is illustrated by views of the (8) Sirinagar Lake in Cashmere, a sheet of water celebrated in song and story; of the town (9) and station of Simla, the summer retreat of the Viceroy and his Council, on the mountain ridge, seeming almost like a city suspended in mid-air, as seen from amidst the foliage of the Jacko Forest; of Mount Everest (10) as seen from the mountainous frontier of Nepaul; of Kinchinjanga (11) from the British hill-station of Darjeeling, these two being the loftiest summits yet discovered in the world.

The fourth Chapter, "The Forest and Wild Sports," is illustrated by views of a tropical forest (12) near the western coast, south of Bombay, with a tarn; and of graceful bamboos (13) hanging over a stream; both places being just the spots whither the tiger comes to slake his thirst.

The fifth Chapter, "The Nationalities and

Religions of India," is illustrated by sketches (14) of a native fair held in tents at a religious festival on the banks of the sacred river Nerbudda, convenient for bathing with all the ceremonies of caste; of a gala company (15) on the stone steps of a sacred tank at Goverdhan, near Mathra, the scene of Hindu religious legends; (16) of the river Ganges, just below Benares, the chief city of the Hindu faith; (17) of a dwelling of the Aborigines in the Nilgherry Hills.

The sixth Chapter, on "The Native States," is illustrated by views of (18) Ambair, near Jyepore, the principal State of Rajputana; of Gwalior (19), a leading Mahratta State; of Hyderabad (20), under a Moslem ruler, held to be the premier native State of India.

The seventh Chapter, on "The Courts and Camps of the Native Princes," is not one that readily admits of illustration according to the method that has been adopted. Still, a sketch has been introduced of the summer-house (21) at Deeg, a native State near Bhurt-pore, not far from the border of Northern

India, perhaps the most perfectly graceful structure of its kind to be found in the Indian Empire; and (22) the Gateway of a Native Palace.

The eighth Chapter, on "The Frontiers of India," has four characteristic views: of the Sikkim-Tibet border (23) in the cold and snowy north; (24) of the Peshawar city, with the Khyber Pass in the background—which was the head and front of the recent frontier campaign—the pools (25) of the stream that runs through the Bolan Pass—leading from the Indus Valley towards Southern Afghanistan; the last two being for the north-west and west, and then of the river Irawady (26) in Burma for the east.

The next two Chapters, the ninth entitled "How India is Governed," the tenth relating to the "Progress of India under British Rule," do not admit of illustration in this manner.

The eleventh Chapter, on "Ruins and Historical Remains," has two illustrations: one relating to the interior of the redstone temple (27) at Bindraban, near Mathra, not far from Agra, being quite the finest interior in any style of architecture throughout India; the other to the great tower at Booddh Gya (28) in Behar, being the stateliest monument remaining to recall the Booddhist era.

The twelfth Chapter, on "Episodes in History and their Localities," is illustrated by a sketch (29) of the Pertabgurh rock-fortress, at the base of which the Mahratta Sivaji assassinated the Moslem envoy, and so set in movement the insurrection of a Hindu nationality against the Moslem Empire; and (30) by a picture of the temple-crowned rock in the midst of the lake at Poona, whence the last of the Peshwas watched his forces being beaten by the British troops, an event which terminated the Mahratta Empire and left it to be succeeded by that of the British.

To the above illustrations have been added (31) one of the Sacred Bull of Tanjore, a granitic monolith, remarkable because the nearest formations of granite are hundreds of miles away; and (32) one of the grey stone temple near Islamabad in Cashmere.

There is yet one more topic to be mentioned at the conclusion of this Preface. After the book had been composed, but before it was completed, certain events occurred, some of which already are affecting India indirectly and may affect her in the future more and more, but of which a notice could not be conveniently included in the body of the work. I allude to the recent development of the British sphere of influence and of commerce in China. Now, without following the ramifications of this immense subject in many directions, all persons connected with India will have observed that one outcome of this affair will be the inclusion of the whole Yangtse River basin in that sphere, at least as far as the rapids and the mountain range which separate the mid-valley of the Yangtse from its upper valley in Czechuen and Yunan. Within the borders of Yunan the river Yangtse is called by British geographers the River of the Golden Sand.

and under that name it approaches the Yunan plateau near Talifoo. This plateau overhangs the valleys of the Mekhong; and the Salwin (as will be seen in Chapter VIII. of this book) touches the Shan States of Burma, belonging to the Empire of India.

Now, from Mandalay, the capital of Ava or Upper Burma, a British railway has been undertaken towards the Chinese frontier in Yunan. Capital has been provided and the project has received the State sanction, for the first part at least. The surveys and other preliminary operations have been or are being conducted as far as the ferry of Kowlong on the Salwin River, which just here is the boundary between the British and the Chinese Empires. Under the circumstances which have arisen in consequence of recent events, it is to be hoped, indeed expected, that the British Government will press on this railway to speedy completion right up to the Salwin. Naturally the line will not stop there, but must eventually be carried on to the Mekhong River and across its basin to the base of the

Yunan plateau. This extension will require the sanction of the Chinese Government. The further enterprise, at the time of the project being initiated, was a matter for negotiations of which the success was more or less doubtful. But in the alteration, indeed the radical improvement, of our relations with China, there should be no longer a doubt as to the success of any arrangements of this nature. Again, this line, with the application of the needful energy and resources, might possibly reach the base of the Yunan plateau in the course of three or four years. But it would not stop there: it must ascend the plateau, which has an altitude of a few thousand feet, by inclines practicable for engineering. Once on the plateau, it would proceed to Talifoo, an important commercial point in the Yunan province. That station would then be within measurable distance of the River of the Golden Sand, which is really the Upper Yangtse. It were premature now to estimate the progress onwards in future years through the Czechuen province towards the mid-valley of the Yangtse, which would be the goal of the long enterprise.

Thus British communications are pressing slowly but, as we hope, surely, on the great Yangtse valley from Shanghai on the east to Mandalay on the west. From Mandalay there is now a railway to Rangoon near the sea. So the main British line of the future, apparently marked out by destiny, is from the Bay of Bengal at Rangoon to the Pacific Ocean near Shanghai, a distance of about three thousand miles right athwart the south-eastern part of the Asiatic continent from sea to sea—one of the finest lines for the march of Empire to be found in all Asia.

CONTENTS

ILLUSTRATIONS

ILLUSTRATIONS

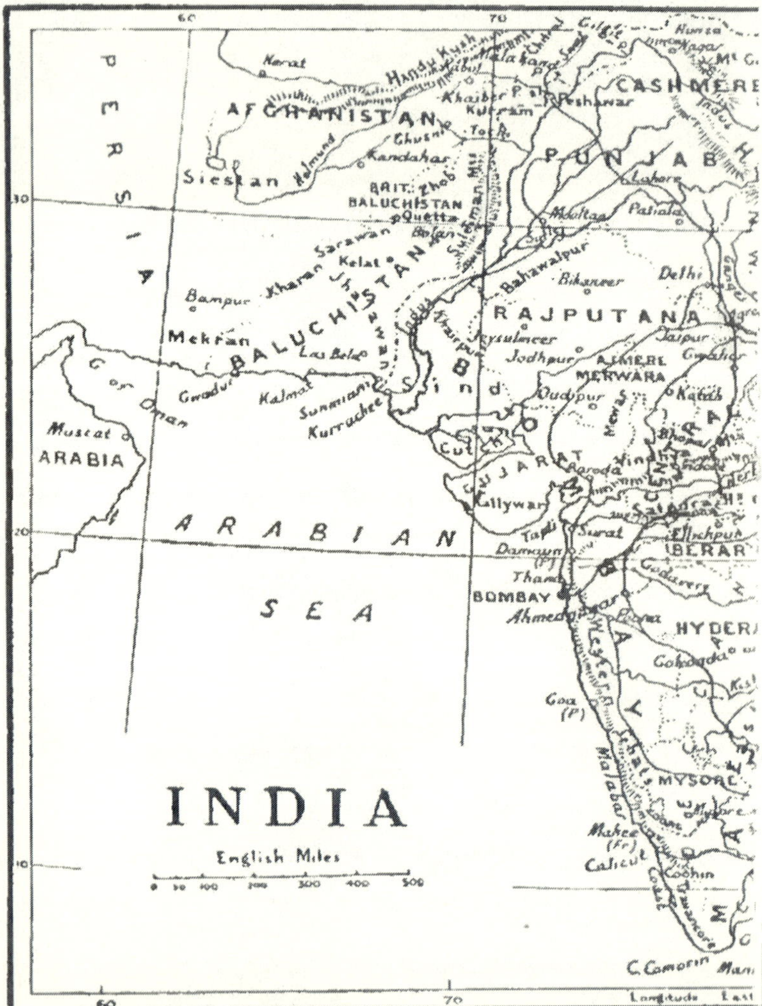

From 'Whitaker's Almanack']

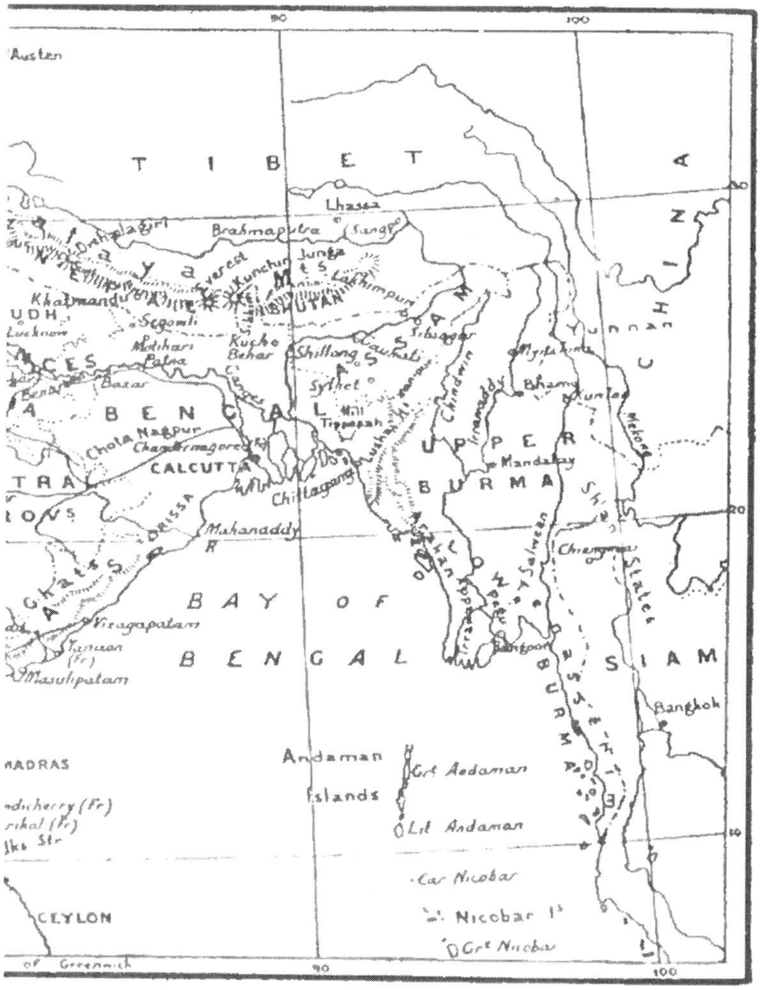

[by permission

CHAPTER I

INTRODUCTORY

India in the Diamond Jubilee year of 1897—Indian troubles in that year—The famine in several provinces—The plague in Bombay—The sedition in Poona—Rioting in Calcutta—Earthquakes in Calcutta and Assam—Uprising of tribes on North-West frontier—Large military operations—Apprehension of national unrest—General improvement in 1898—Closure of the Mints, and question of silver currency.

I PROPOSE to give some account of India in her romantic and picturesque aspects. In no year since the beginning of British rule has she been more prominently before English eyes than in 1897. The Diamond Jubilee of the Queen Empress brought many of the native representatives to England. Though not native Sovereigns of the first rank, many of them were native Princes, others were nobles; and many were soldiers, no doubt carefully chosen by the Government of India for their martial bearing, their war-record, their social status, in addition to military rank. Certainly they represented India handsomely and gracefully. They gave to Englishmen a favourable idea of the inherent manliness and of the true gentility pertaining to the best classes of native society. They doubtless inspired many of our countrymen with a desire to know more, and if possible to see something of the land whence these people came. They suggested by their presence the thought that the birthplace of such picturesque figures must in itself be replete with pictorial effect.

But this ideal mind-picture of India in 1897 has had—like realistic and material pictures —its deep shades as well as its high lights. For few years have seen such long and ever lengthening shadows been cast right across India from end to end as the year just passed, namely, 1897. These sorrows sprang upon her just at the zenith of her strength, her prosperity, and her splendour. This was indeed providentially fortunate, inasmuch as the burden fell upon her at a time when she was fairly able to bear it. The year opened with one of the severest and most widespread famines ever known, extending over various provinces in Northern and Western India, and in several districts elsewhere. India has always been the land of famine, arising from atmospheric causes of a far-reaching character quite beyond human control. For now nearly two generations the British Government has striven to prevent famine by constructing works of irrigation, the finest known in any age or country. But prevention by these means is found to be impracticable though the possible area is contracted. Still during the same era Government has devoted its energies and resources to averting or mitigating the consequences of drought and dearth. On this dread occasion the Indian people faced the calamity with all the old endurance for which, indeed, they have been proverbial. The Government combated the sufferings with all the old resourcefulness and administrative capacity for which it has been famous. The sympathies of England were aroused, and the subscriptions for relief of famine exceeded half a million sterling, the largest sum, or one of the largest sums, ever raised for a charity of this description. These effort in the British Isles, and in India itself under British auspices, were beginning to prove successful, and were blessed by such improvement in the season as gave hope of a speedy recovery, when a new trouble was added in the shape of plague and pestilence.

During the spring the plague appeared sporadically in Western India, and then became for a while endemic in Bombay, decimating the inhabitants in some quarters of the great city, and causing such an exodus of the busy population as to paralyse for a while the industry of this queen of Asiatic commerce. This was on the coast at the foot of the Western Ghaut Mountains. Then the plague crossed the mountains and appeared at Poona, a great civil and military station, and the capital of the Bombay Deccan. Meanwhile the Government of Bombay had been doing its utmost to check the evil, by internal sanitation in dwellings, by disinfecting processes, by isolation of distressed localities, and so forth. This benevolent work, designed solely to save the lives and to promote the health of the people, was introduced at first in Bombay and soon extended to Poona.

Then at Poona certain persons pretended that this good work was vexatious and oppressive. On this particular ground the people were urged by seditious publications to rebel. Two meritorious English officers were actually murdered on this very pretence, and the murderers were not at the time discovered.

Soon it became evident that the treason went further and deeper. Newspaper articles were published invoking the memory of the national hero Sivaji, who more than two centuries ago raised the standard of Hindu revolt against the Great Mogul. With an eloquence peculiarly appealing to the Hindu mind, the people of to-day were urged to treat the British in the same way. At least to the British understanding this was the substance and tenor of the admonition. All this was done not at all by ordinary natives but by men who had been at our schools and colleges and had studied at our University in Bombay. At first sight it was most discouraging to see such an outcome of Western civilisation. There had been mutterings of the storm for some time in the native press. After long-suffering patience, which had perhaps been too far protracted, the Government acted with its wonted energy. Criminal prosecutions were instituted; several natives of social consequence were brought to the bar and received judicial sentence. These proceedings checked the publication of seditious and treasonable matter. Hardly any overt act of rebellion occurred. But nobody supposed that the inflammable material had been removed, although the rising flame had been stamped out. Indeed those who, like myself, are thoroughly acquainted with that locality and with the people concerned, know well that in and about Poona there resides in some bosoms an inextinguishable hatred against

British rule,— implacable notwithstanding humane legislation, just laws and honest administration.

Thus in the summer, just when England was ringing with the Jubilee cheers, when the colonies and dependencies from every clime were swelling the chorus of congratulation, when the inhabitants of the British Isles were giving munificent proofs of sympathy with their Asiatic fellow-subjects, when the Indian Government was signalising itself by immense efforts for the sake of suffering humanity, treasonable symptoms of the worst kind manifested themselves in Western India. Never was mischief of this sort more ill-timed. The people of England were perhaps too much absorbed in the Imperial triumphs of the moment to pay close attention to the matter. But they thought it dangerous, and wondered why this time of all other times should be chosen for such manifestations. This wonderment of theirs is shared indeed by those who are most experienced in these affairs. The truth probably is that in that particular quarter the discontent is abiding, and only awaits any chance event that may seem to promise an opportunity. It was thought by the evil disposed that such an opportunity might be afforded by the dissatisfaction, real or supposed, of the people, at the measures taken for the prevention of the plague. Never was benevolent effort more unjustly misunderstood.

But the apprehension of people in England regarding these events soon became quickened. For rioting, not amounting to rebellion, but still most grave, broke out very soon in Calcutta. A dispute arose about a building and some land claimed for a mosque, regarding which a judicial decree had been issued. The affair was small, but the mob became great, and the rioting spread largely before the authorities were able, by the employment of troops, to put it down. After these events, first on the west, then on the east side of India, rumour came in with its hundred tongues. Insolence of demeanour before Europeans, ominous expressions casually dropped, were commonly reported ; and no doubt many Europeans, who ought to be well-informed, did think that an unaccountable spirit of unrest was in the air. As this became known in England some genuine alarm was felt by many Englishmen. It was graphically depicted in an eminent London weekly journal by an illustration of the tiger. I often heard them ask whether there was not going to be another Mutiny, alluding of course to 1857. This would presuppose or imply some sinister signs in the native army. But in truth in 1897 there was not the slightest trace of this. On the contrary, the native army was sorely tried during this very year, and evinced the most gallant loyalty.

Then another physical calamity supervened. Earthquake shook parts of Calcutta, and appeared with still greater force in the valley of the Brahmaputra, underneath the eastern Himalayas, threatening the tea-producing regions. The station of Shillong in Assam was nearly destroyed. India is indeed a buoyant country ; still this recurrence of calamity must have caused some gloom to settle down on the public mind.

Immediately, however, a new excitement arose in a widely different and distant part of the country. Far away on the North-West frontier, near Peshawar, and round about the celebrated Khyber Pass that leads towards Caubul, there was an uprising of the independent tribes that occupy a long though narrow belt of mountains between the Indus valley and Afghanistan. It was found that fanatical Moslem priests had been stirring up all these wild and intractable tribesmen to resist, and if possible drive back, what were considered the British encroachments on their territories. Whether this fanaticism had anything to do with current events in Europe relating to the Sultan of Turkey had never been ascertained exactly. At any rate the movement grew and grew, not only in extent, but in vigour and organisation, till it became the biggest affair of its kind ever known on that famous frontier during the half century of British connection with it, say, since 1849. Uprisings of this kind—attacks really upon British outposts or upon British villages near the base of the mountain-line—have during the half-century been chronic, that is, ever-recurring from time to time, and are expected to be so. The region has long been known favourably in military circles as a capital school for soldiers, both European and native. We have always acknowledged and respected the independence of these tribes within their own borders—that is, their mountains. Practically, they have never been quite satisfied with that, and would like to lord it over the fertile tracts near the foot of the hills—tracts which never were their territories, but which belonged to the Punjab kingdom before us, and to us since 1849. Doubtless we have protected our own ground, and punished invasions of it more effectively than our predecessors ever did. Hence the several frontier expeditions, some twenty-five or thirty in number within the fifty years, always of a punitive character, of which the world has heard from time to time. These have always been short, sharp, and successful, without ever attaining any considerable dimensions. They have generally been settled with our native troops only, and with the employment of Europeans in small numbers or not at all. But this uprising in 1897 was a far larger and more formidable affair, requiring a whole army corps, with a goodly proportion of European troops. Indeed, according to some calculations, the forces employed, including those in the front and those in reserve, amounted to two army corps. It really constituted something like a new departure in frontier history. It was not concluded within the year 1897; but early in the next year, 1898, the conclusion was held to have been attained by the submission of the last of the insurgent tribes. Hereafter this grave case will need thorough examination as regards the past, the present, and the future. Suffice to say that the conflict—though ushered in by fanaticism—raged mainly in reference to the occupation and guardianship of certain passes, notably among them the Khyber Pass, leading from the Indus valley into Afghanistan, which the Government of India claim the right of guarding in the interests of the Empire. At first it was thought that the occupation of Chitral might have been at the bottom of the affair, but this is now found not to be the case. The Chitral tribes have been either friendly or quiescent. The insurgents belong to other tribes with different objects in view. Still the wonder remains as to how these tribes, heretofore separate in their conduct and in their objects, should on this occasion have combined in such large numbers for one or two common objects. Inquiry has probably yet to be completed as to what these objects were. At present I believe they relate mainly to the passes. I will not now pursue this subject, save to remark that nothing could be better than the behaviour of the native troops of the British army throughout these arduous operations. In this work, too, some of the troops of the native Princes of the Empire have had an honourable share.

India always has been a land of peril, of calamity, and of emergency, despite all her splendid advantages. In British history she has gone through two awful years, 1857 and 1858, the like of which we, the witnesses, in part or in whole, hope never to see again. Still for a time of peace, of general prosperity, of political success, the year 1897 has been an *annus mirabilis*. Famine, plague, earthquake, treasonable sedition, rioting, frontier warfare—occurred one after the other, all within a few months. So to speak, the curtain has fallen on one scene only to rise on another. But in the following year, 1898, a large part, though not the whole, of these clouds passed away from the political sky. The seasonable rains not only relieved famine, but even ensured plenty. Quiet was restored on the North-West frontier. The plague-stricken population of Bombay did indeed resume their industries with renewed health. But in the spring of 1898 there was a recrudescence of the plague, and soon the pestilence appeared in Calcutta, in Kurrachee, and other places. The consequences of this devastation are still severely felt.

With all these extraordinary occurrences India failed to share fully in the Jubilee joyousness which reigned in all other parts of the British Empire. Still, in the following year, 1898, she retrieved much of her passing misfortunes, and she still stands socially erect.

Besides these actual dangers or misfortunes there was one threatened danger from which India has been preserved by the firmness of the Government in India and in England. For some time past, by closing its mints to coinage of silver, the Government of India has sustained the exchange rate of the rupee at a certain standard which is compatible with the safety of the Indian finances and of other great interests connected therewith. Certain proposals came from the United States of America, which were, indeed, designed for improving the value of silver, but which involved the reopening of the Indian mints to coinage. By the rejection of these proposals India was saved from financial peril at a time of exceptional suffering and trouble. But the anxiety was renewed in the following year, 1898, and the whole subject is under inquiry by the Government in England.

I have deemed it necessary to recount these circumstances of 1897, as largely alleviated in 1898, before describing India as she is in all her beauty. They could not, indeed, be properly passed over in silence; if they were, then my survey might be deemed optimistic. A description of India to be true must be bright and cheerful, but the interest is enhanced by remembering that behind the brightness and cheerfulness there ever lurks danger and possible disaster. Still, the dangers are always overcome and the disasters retrieved. On the other hand, any gloomy or pessimistic description of India is sure to be wrong. If my picture shall be rightly painted the lights and the shadows must be duly apportioned, though, as in other bright pictures, the lights will be dominant.

CHAPTER II

A WINTER'S TOUR IN INDIA

Tour begins at Bombay—Trip to Goojerat and Kattywar—Return to Bombay and start for Northern India—Visit to Oodeypore and Jyepore in Rajputana—Gwalior and entry to Hindostan—Agra and Delhi—The Panjab—Umritsur and Lahore—The Indus and Peshawar—Return to Hindostan—The Ganges Canal—Cawnpore, Lucknow, and Benares—Calcutta—Thence across the Continent to Nagpore—To Poona and Mahabuleshwar—Hyderabad in the Deccan—To Madras, Vellore, and Arcot—Trichinopoly—The Nilgherry Mountains—The Southern Peninsula—Madura and Tinnevelly—Then by Ceylon homewards.

WHEN entering on the field of Indian picturesqueness I feel like one who looks on some vast collection of beautiful objects, say the National Gallery or Kew Gardens, and knows not where to begin his survey. But in order to make my summary—for it cannot be more — both practical and popular, I shall conduct the reader in imagination through the Grand Tour of India—thus touching on most of the finest points in the country.

Such a tour is being made more and more frequently year after year by increasing numbers of English ladies and gentlemen. The ladies generally return with their spirits enlivened, and the range of their imagination much widened. The gentlemen come back full of ideas derived from knowledge which is real so far as it goes, provided that they do not think too much of the knowledge they have thus acquired, and suppose themselves to know more than could possibly be known on a very short acquaintance. They benefit immensely by the journey in mental strength and in the grasp of Imperial affairs. It is satisfactory, too, that they always seem to be deeply impressed by the organisation of British rule in the country.

The tour I am about to sketch must be made in the winter, the climate renders this obligatory. The winter in India is finer even than that of the Riviera, or of Southern Italy. The spring and summer are so hot as to be prohibitory, and the autumn is unhealthy. Therefore the tourist must leave England by the first weekly overland mail of October, so as to break ground at Bombay by November 1. Then he may well remain in India till the first homeward mail in April. Thus he would have five months, November, December, January, February, March, for his tour, which, if really well directed, is one of the most magnificent that can be taken on earth. I shall suggest the line or lines that can best be followed, premising that I have myself been to all the places which will be recommended, and that with many of them I have had long and intimate acquaintance.

I shall, however, have to touch but very lightly on each place, passing always quickly, as on a rapid tour, the country being a flowery mead, where the traveller, like a gay butterfly, flits from flower to flower.

At Bombay, the western capital, the tourist would have no time to stop and examine the various institutions, unless, indeed, there might be some particular, say, educational, institution in which he took an interest, and which could be looked at in two or three hours. But he should make sure of seeing from some point on Malabar Hill, say Malabar Point, the Governor's Marine Villa, the long and magnificent series of public buildings, one of the finest sights of its kind in the world. The buildings are in themselves grand, but other cities may have structures as grand, though probably separate. Bombay, however, has all her structures in one long line of array, as if on parade before the spectator. And all this is right over the blue bay, with the Western Ghaut Mountains in the distant background. This constitutes a noble introduction for the traveller to picturesque India.

Then we pass through the vast harbour of Bombay, with a comparatively narrow mouth, guarded by fortifications, surrounded

DISTANT VIEW OF BOMBAY HARBOUR

by hills, and studded with islands—again with a mountain background. This harbour is in the very first rank of the harbours of the world, taking an equal place with Sydney, with San Francisco, with Rio de Janeiro. The immediate purpose is, however, to visit the island of Elephanta in the inner part of the harbour and see the Cave temples, rock-hewn chambers, with massive figures and antique devices, offering a wondrous spectacle to a new-comer from the Western world.

Then the traveller should determine on broad considerations the route he is going to take from one end to the other of the Indian continent. There are, of course, several alternatives, but the one which I shall adopt is as follows. First, let us proceed through Goojerat to Ahmedabad—with a possible diversion to the cluster of native States in Kattywar—and back to Bombay; a trip of only two or three days. The traveller would thus see the most fertile coast region in India, with some wonderful railway bridges over deltaic rivers, and some strange specimens of Moslem architecture, unique of its kind. It would be well to make this excursion, which is easily made now, but for the making of which no opportunity will recur.

Returning to Bombay, the traveller should start at once for the distant Panjab, by way of Central India and Rajputana. The railway would carry him to the foot of the Western Ghaut Mountains, not far from the new waterworks, with a dam, probably the most massive in the world ; then up the mountain sides to Nassik and onwards near Asirgurh, the imposing hill fortress dominating this part of the main line between Bombay and Calcutta. Descending into the valley of the Nerbudda, and, crossing that river, he would ascend the Vindhya Mountains and reach, near Indore, the great cluster of native States which is called Central India. There is nothing to detain him at or near Indore, unless he should be able to spare two days or so to visit the fine ruins of Mandu, once a city with a stately court and camp, but now, since some centuries, a typical instance of absolute desolation. From Indore he might, if possible, diverge to Oodeypore, the noblest of all the Rajput States, which is signalised by the architecture of its palaces overlooking lakes. Thence he would proceed to Jeypore, the wealthiest of the Rajput States. The laying out of the modern capital is a good instance of native skill. But even more interesting is the old and half deserted capital at Ambair, full of good specimens of ancient Rajput architecture in the Hindu style, both as regards palaces and fortifications. Then he may pass by Gwalior, belonging to Sindhia, the first among the Mahratta States, and a striking instance of those natural fortresses formed by rock masses rising abruptly out of the plains, in which India abounds. Then he would cross the river Jamna and enter Hindostan.

The plain of Hindostan—the upper basin of the Jamna and the Ganges—is the most important part of India, the scene of Hindu sacred legends, the Imperial seat of the Great Mogul. The traveller soon arrives at Agra, to contemplate the red sandstone palace-fortress of Akber the Great, the first of the Great Moguls, with its "pearl-mosque," resplendent in white marble against the azure sky. He stands in the balcony whence the dying Emperor Shah Jehan took a last look at the distant Taj Mehal, the peerless mausoleum which he had erected for his dead Empress. A short drive takes the tourist to the Taj Mehal, the shrine which has immortalised a Mogul Empress, the finest instance of architecture in marble ever known, superb in its swelling dome, in the proportions of its structure, in the climatic conditions which have preserved the loveliness of its material almost unimpaired, and by common consent the queen of beauty among all structures in the world. Thence he soon journeys to Delhi, the opening scene of the tragedy of the mutinies in 1857. Again he sees a red sandstone palace-fortress overlooking the Jamna, and close by the Jama Mosque, in the magnitude of its

TAJ MEHAL, FROM AGRA FORTRESS

LAHORE CITADEL

style and its material, red sandstone picked out with marble, the finest mosque ever erected in the many regions over which the faith of Islam has spread. He drives over the remains of dead cities, and realises that there have been several Delhis close by, and before the present Delhi. After reverently contemplating the ridge before Delhi, the scene of British heroism and endurance during the memorable siege of 1857, during the Mutinies, he sets his face straight for the river Satlej and enters the Panjab.

On his way to Lahore he may stop a few hours at Umritsur to see the gilded temple in the midst of a lake—the headquarters of the Sikh religion. At Lahore, the capital of the Panjab, he would pause briefly to notice the city walls and the mosques, again remarkable for their material, among which may be reckoned the colours of the earth-enamel, matchlessly beautiful, the product of an art now lost. He will observe the comparatively modern tomb of Ranjit Sing, the Lion of the

Panjab, the founder of a kingdom which made the Sikhs a nation.

Thence he would hurry northwards, crossing by mighty railway viaducts the Chenab and the Jhelum, and recalling the marches of Alexander the Great, till he reached the Indus at Attok, the most celebrated of the river crossings in India. This has always been an Imperial point in the history of many Asiatic dynasties, and he will find the swift river rockbound between lofty sides, in its weird picturesqueness worthy of its historic renown. Soon the railway carries him to Peshawur, which, though full of prestige and celebrity, has few objects of interest. But a short ride will take him near to the mouth of the Khyber Pass, close enough for a glance into the gloomy portals between India and Afghanistan.

By this time he will probably feel the difference between the sharp bracing climate with frosty nights, and the mild moist atmosphere as felt when he landed in India. The whole of this vast distance he will have accomplished by railway within a very few weeks. During his passage through the Panjab he may, at lucky moments in favouring weather, have caught glimpses of the snowy range of the Himalayas.

He must now quickly retrace his steps towards Hindostan, not, however, returning to Delhi, but bearing to the north and nearing the Himalayas near Deyrah Dhoon. If he should have leisure to diverge, for two days or so, to Hardwar to visit the engineering works at the head of the Ganges Canal—the finest works of their kind in the world, seen, too, with a mountainous background — he would do well. But he may not have time. So he would hasten on through the Gangetic valley, to Cawnpore, not itself remarkable for anything save the pathetic monument over the well where the British victims of the mutinies found the rudest of tombs. He would there consider whether he has time to diverge for two days or so to Lucknow, a place illustrious in British annals, but not externally remarkable, inasmuch as its Moslem architecture is second-rate, and will appear to be utterly inferior after the superb examples he has been seeing at Agra, Delhi, and Lahore. At all events he must proceed past Allahabad, at the confluence of the Ganges and the Jamna, and the largest junction station in India, to Benares. A day or two days he must give to Benares, the capital city of the Hindu faith. Passing gently down the stream of the Ganges in a boat he sees the finest river frontage in India—a long series of palaces and conical temples with flights of stone steps down the steep bank to the river, crowded with persons pressing onwards to dip in the sacred water. If he desires to study Christian Missions, now is the time and here is the place for this purpose.

He must now make a straight run by railway to Calcutta, not pausing much at the Imperial capital with its many institutions. Still he will notice Dalhousie Square, a small lake surrounded by public buildings—the finest square in India—the long lines of structures, public and private, facing the great

EDEN GARDENS, CALCUTTA

TEMPLE AT NAGPORE

green plain, the Eden Gardens on the Hooghly bank alongside the ocean-going ships, the broad river filled with shipping like the Pool of the Thames. He has now reached the limit of his grand tour, and will henceforward be on his way home.

From Calcutta he should make a straight cut across the country to Nagpore, in the very heart of India, by the railway which has in recent years been constructed. Heretofore his railway journeys will have taken him across mountain ranges and along never ending plains, verdant with the young rising crops of the cool season. But now he will, from his carriage windows, obtain some idea of the forests and jungles of India. From Nagpore—the capital of the Central Provinces, at which place there is little save Mahratta structures of some beauty and interest to detain him—he should proceed through Berar to the Bombay Deccan *en route* to Poona. If he could spare two days or so to visit the rock-hewn temples, commonly called the caves of Ajunta, he would do well, especially as he would hardly have time to visit the sister caves of Ellora. These gloomy chambers in the heart of the black rock formations, with statues and images of the grandest designs, are of unique interest. Poona is replete with historic associations as the old headquarters of the Mahratta Confederation, whose empire in India was superseded by that of the British. It is also fraught with grave political considerations at the present time. But it has few sights to offer, except the lake with the temple-crowned rock in the midst.

Here again the traveller would do well if he could spare four days or so in order to diverge to Mahabuleshwar, the summer residence of the Bombay Presidency. The scenery is wondrous, with the vast face of the mountain range and the mighty walls of laminated rock right over the coast region with the Indian Ocean on the western horizon. Prominent in the view is the square tower-like hill of Pertabgarh, where two centuries and a half ago Sivaji, the Mahratta, by assassinating the Moslem envoy, raised the standard of Hindu revolt against the Muhammadan Empire.

Returning to Poona the traveller may proceed to Hyderabad, the Nizam's capital. The sights at Hyderabad, gateways, mosques, and the like, are fine, but hardly in the first rank, and in the Nizam's Palace there is nothing to see. Still, he would gather some idea of the pomp and state, the court and camp, the political and social atmosphere of the largest among all the native States of India. He might devote one day to Golconda, called the City of Tombs, because it contains the mausoleum of an entire Moslem dynasty.

From Hyderabad he should proceed to Madras. There is not much, save the public structures and the new harbour, to detain him in this, the capital of Southern India. But he will proceed, passing by Vellore and Arcot, memorable for those contests of the last century which decided the question whether the Empire of India should go to the French or to the English. So he will reach the foot of the Nilgherry Mountains, the summer resort of the Madras Presidency, and ascend to the plateau of Octacamund. From these heights he will survey an ocean of lower hills, rising and diminishing just like billows, with the Nilgherry—literally blue peak—towering aloft, and the shimmer of the Indian Ocean on the horizon.

Descending to the plain, which has now become the Southern Peninsula, he will visit the Rock of Trichinopoly, famous in the record of British heroism, and the noble temples of Tanjore. He would have a glimpse, too, of the magnificent system of irrigation in that region. Still journeying southwards he reaches Madura, containing unsurpassed examples of Hindu sacred architecture. He might possibly make a diversion to Travancore, with luxuriant vegetation, but probably there would not be time for this. Further to the south he would visit the Christian Protestant missions in Tinnevelly, the field where Christianity

TRICHINOPOLY ROCK

has most widely spread among the natives, and has most firmly taken root. Thence he would soon reach the southern extremity of India, and crossing over to Ceylon would embark at Colombo by some mail steamer bound for England.

I must allow that by this programme of travel, the Marble Rocks at Jubbulpore, which constitute one of the natural gems of India, would be omitted. The only remedy would be to visit them by an excursion from Nagpore, for which, however, there might not be time. The great irrigation works on the east coast have not been included. But time might be found for visiting them from Madras, if the traveller should feel a special interest in the subject.

If this programme, this itinerary, this projected tour, were accomplished in the five months, it would constitute a grand record of travel. I believe that it could be done, provided that the traveller were not tempted to linger anywhere unduly. But comprehensive as its scope may be, it unavoidably omits

Sind and Burma, and also the river-kingdom of Eastern Bengal with Assam.

Finally it does not touch the grand region of the Himalayas, of which I shall treat in the next chapter.

CHAPTER III

A SUMMER'S SOJOURN IN THE HIMALAYA

Journey through India from Ceylon to the base of Himalaya in the Panjab—Approach Cashmere by Bara-Moolla Pass—Scenery of Cashmere—Leave it by the Bannihal Pass—Jammu State—Kangra hill fort and Dharmsala Valley—Simla and its circumstances—Lake of Naini Tal—Darjeeling and the Snowy Range—Frontier of Tibet—Conclusion of tour either by the Irawady River and Burma—Or by the Indus and the Bolan Pass.

THE last preceding chapter on the winter's tour on the continent of India did not include the Himalaya. The name Himalaya is Sanskrit, meaning "the abode of snow." On such a tour some glimpses of the Himalaya may occasionally be had. But a visit to the Himalaya cannot be combined with a tour on the Indian continent, because it must not be made in the winter.

During that season the region is under snow, and to attempt a visit then would be like visiting the higher Alpine districts in January! Nevertheless the Himalaya, though not geographically belonging to the Indian continent, is technically a part of India—has been in all the ages looked up to with sacred awe by the Hindus as the celestial abode, and is the most grandly picturesque part of the whole British Empire. Therefore the English traveller should by all means visit it, if he can. But in that case he must make up his mind to a year's stay in India—leaving England in October of one year and returning towards the end of the following year. When thinking of a journey to India English travellers often say that they would above all places like to see Cashmere. Yes, certainly it is one of the places best worth seeing in the world, but this cannot be included in the winter's tour. As it is inside the Himalaya, a visit to it would involve a whole year in India as already explained.

At all events the Himalaya cannot be

excluded from the survey of Picturesque India. But differing as it does from the continent of India proper in most though not all respects, it had better be treated separately. For this purpose I will suppose that the traveller had decided to visit the Himalaya together with India and is prepared to give the year's time that would be required. In that case it would be best for him to take in reverse, so to speak, the grand tour sketched in the last article. Or better still let him proceed to Colombo, arriving there very early in November—instead of Bombay—and thence cross to Southern India, taking Tinnevelly, Madura, Trichinopoly, and the Nilgherries, to Madras. Thence he will proceed by Hyderabad and Poona to Bombay. After a brief stay in Bombay he would proceed straight to Calcutta through Berar and Nagpore. From Calcutta he would work his way up the Gangetic valley by Benares, Agra and Delhi to the Panjab — then through the Panjab by Lahore to Peshawar. By this time the tour will have occupied the winter, and the spring will be advancing. Returning from Peshawar and recrossing the Indus at Attock, he would stop for a moment at Rawalpindi not far off at the base of the Himalaya—say about the end of March. The various localities above mentioned have been already touched upon in the preceding chapter.

From Rawalpindi he may begin his tour in the Himalaya, remembering that the places to be seen in one summer are many and that there will be very little time for marching amidst the mountains or for pursuing sport. If any time be given to sport it must be deducted from the tour. If the traveller becomes for a while a sportsman he will indeed see some parts of the Himalaya extremely well, but he will fail to make any round of the Himalaya as a whole.

Let us suppose then that he breaks ground at Rawalpindi, not far from the Indus, in the very beginning of April, and rides up to Murri, the principal summer resort for the European society of the Panjab. The season will not have begun and the place will be comparatively empty; but he will have his first introduction to Himalayan scenery, at an altitude of 6000 to 8000 feet above sea level. He will see more of forests than of rocks, but will be struck by the true Himalaya, or abode of snow, a line of snowy peaks looking as if massed together like one long white wall against the sky, and trending towards Cashmere, his immediate goal. From Murri he marches a short way into the mountains, and then makes a sharp and steep descent to the valley of the Jhelum. He follows the course of this river upstream for a few daily marches to the Bara-Moolla Pass. Emerging from this pass he finds himself in an upland plateau surrounded by mountains, with an extensive vista looking eastwards, and, lo, this is the Vale of Cashmere, of which the main artery is the river Jhelum. The wondering delight of every traveller on first beholding Cashmere is proverbial. The valley may be and often is approached by other routes besides that of the

Bara-Moolla. But this latter is the only one by which it can be entered so early in the season as the beginning of April. The fair region is essentially a valley of lakes ; so he first sees the largest of these lakes, and then, following the course of the Jhelum, pushes on to Sirinagar, the capital, built, like Venice, on canals, and having a lake of consummate beauty, on the margin of which the Great Moguls built their summer palaces. These are the sweet spots of which the poet Moore had dreamt when he sung his "Lalla Rookh." Here the traveller should ascend the hill, Takht-i-Suleman (Solomon's Throne), which juts out from the main range, standing a thousand feet or more above the valley. The panorama seen from this lofty standpoint is never forgotten. The whole of Cashmere, encircled by snowy ranges, is spread out below the eye. Such a complete environment of snow-clad summits, along all the four quarters of the compass, is rarely or never to be seen elsewhere. The traveller will pursue his journey, in a prettily furnished barge on the Jhelum towed upstream, to Islamabad, where he will land in order to visit the famous Hindu ruins. Thence he will cross to the eastern end of the valley to the lovely fountain of Vernag, welling up from the base of the mountains and being the reputed source of the Jhelum.

The season will by this time be sufficiently advanced for him to leave the valley from this end by what is called the Bunnihal route across the Chenab river to Jammu.

From this Bunnihal route some distant views of the central snowy ranges will be obtained—several lines of snow at varying distances. Then the traveller begins to realise the breadth of the Himalaya. He is close, indeed, to snowy mountains, but they are only the lesser ranges—the outworks, as it were, of the central range. He descends to the river Chenab, which rolls along as a young giant through the mountains. He reascends to some lofty plateaux and descends again to Jammu, the capital of the kingdom—that is, of the native State of Jammu-Cashmere. This place is finely situated near a three-peaked hill, called by the natives the Triple-headed Goddess. Here is an opportunity of studying a Himalayan native Prince with his picturesque surroundings.

The traveller must now revert to the plains of the Punjab, skirting as near as he can the base of the mountains, and crossing the fine irrigation works of the Bari Doab canal, till he reaches Kot Kangra, a rock citadel and one of the most characteristic of the Himalayan hill-fortresses. Then he ascends the mountains, and reaches the valley of Dharmsala, a marvellous expanse of rice culture conducted with countless irrigation channels from the hill-streams around. This perfect garden is surrounded by forest-clad hills, above which rise the snowy peaks. Such a spectacle is almost unique, even in the Himalayas. The traveller must now again revert to the plains of the Panjab until he reaches the river Sutlej. There he takes the railway train to Umballa at the foot of the Simla hills.

Ascending the mountains by the Simla

road, he soon reaches Kussowlee, some 6000 feet above sea-level. He looks back over the vast plain of the Sutlej basin which he has just quitted and which commands a wondrous prospect. The apparently limitless expanse of land looks like the ocean, the distant horizon melting into the sky. The curves of the winding Sutlej and its affluents form a fitting contrast to the horizontal lines of the landscape. This view of the plains, from a mountain rising aloft immediately over them, is most remarkable. Before quitting the Himalaya we shall find more views of this nature. They are certainly the most striking landscape scenes in India, and must be in the first rank among the views of this kind in the world.

Near Kussowlee is Dugshai, and both stations are occupied by European troops. The traveller will notice that these stations, in combination with Umballa, form a reserve of European strength for North-Western India.

By this time the month of May will be

advancing and the season for Simla begun. The Viceroy and his Government, with some of the official classes, will have arrived and the world of Anglo-Indian fashion will have assembled. The traveller then may well halt here for awhile and contemplate this summer resort of the Government of India and its surroundings, including the army headquarters. Owing to the extension of railway facilities, the families of officers, military and civil, can easily betake themselves to the mountains, which are cool, while the plains have by this time become burning hot. Consequently Simla has now become bright with ladies, and the social gatherings on the green swards, underneath the rocks, overshadowed by the fir, the pine, the cedar, are of daily occurrence. The rich bloom of the rhododendrons lends gorgeousness to the scene. The place is like a gay Swiss city isolated on the mountain top—with dark ilex forests around it, blue hills beyond, the horizon being ever whitened by the snowy range. The town almost seeming to be suspended between heaven

HILL STATION OF SIMLA

and earth! There are but few wheeled conveyances; when guests are bidden to balls and parties, the ladies go in Sedan chairs with gaily clad bearers and the gentlemen ride on hill ponies. But in this paradise, tempting the mind to banish care and forget affairs of State, the most arduous business is daily even hourly conducted. Red liveried messengers are running to and fro all the day and half the night. Tons of weight of letters and despatches come and go daily. Here are gathered up the threads of an Empire. Hence issue the orders affecting perhaps one-sixth of the human race. The traveller may pause for a time to observe in close juxtaposition all that is loveliest on the face of Nature and all that is most strenuous in the life of man. He should take a really good look at Simla in all its peculiarities, being well assured that there is no other place like it in the world.

Before the rains begin in the middle of June he should make at least one short excursion from Simla into the interior, and for this purpose must be prepared for some hard marching. The best of these is that to the summit of the Chôre Mountain, about 12,000 or 13,000 feet above sea level. He should be awake and seated outside his little tent before dawn to watch the sun rising behind the snowy range and gradually gilding the famous peaks—like three gables and a cathedral tower—whose glaciers supply the sources of the sacred rivers, the Ganges and the Jamna. He may reflect on the millions of devout Hindu eyes which are turned towards these distant peaks from the plains far below with superstitious awe or with affectionate reverence.

When the rains of June shall have cooled the weather in the plains the traveller must descend from Simla to Umballa, and take the railway to a point near the base of the mountains of Naini Tal, the summer resort for the North Western Provinces, and, as the name Tal implies, the leading feature is a lovely lake embosomed in the mountains. If the weather should permit he might make an excursion to the uplands of Almora, whence a magnificent array of snowy peaks is visible.

Thus the rainy reason passes and he must again seek the plains, which are now traversed by swollen rivers in full flood. He will travel by rail along the Behar lowlands to Northern Bengal, and so ascend the eastern Himalaya to Darjeeling, the queen of Himalayan beauty. He would thus reach it in the early autumn, when the veil and curtain of cloud masses and rolling vapours have been uplifted to display the peerless snows in all the gilding of Oriental sunshine. Looking upwards to the snows of Kinchinjunga and downwards to the valley depths, he takes in 26,000 feet of altitude (nearly double the height of Mont Blanc) in one sweep of the eye. Nowhere in the Himalayas will he find the foreground so rich as here—owing to the longitude as well as the latitude the vegetation is semi-tropical—the airy fairy tree-fern, and the flowering magnolia are in the front, while the everlasting snows are piercing the sky. If possible he should take two excursions, one to a neighbouring range, where he would find the largest rhododendrons yet known to botany, and in the distance Mount Everest, which, with Kinchinjanga, forms the loftiest pair of mountains yet discovered in the world, between 28,000 and 29,000 feet above sea level. His other excursion would be to the chain of beautiful lakes, from 13,000 to 14,000 feet above sea level, on the frontier of Sikkim, forming the boundary between India and Tibet.

He would then descend to the deltaic region of Bengal, as autumn is advancing apace, re-visit Calcutta, and take steamer to England.

But if he can give another fortnight, he might well pay a flying visit to Burma, see the Rangoon gilded pagoda shooting up like a flame of fire into the air, the banks of the Irawady, the teak wood-carving and the gilded finials of Prome forming one vast pyramid, the gigantic images of Booddha with his transcendental and sublime dignity, the panorama of Moulmein with three rivers flowing (two

MOUNT EVEREST

MOUNT KINCHINJANGA

from the hills of Siam) into the bay of Martaban.

Or he might re-cross India by the Nagpore route to Bombay, thence proceed by sea to Kurrachi and the Lower Indus to Sukkur. Then he might by rail proceed to the British frontier adjoining South Afghanistan, visiting the Bolan Pass, and returning to Kurrachi, from which port he would embark for England.

The grand tour of the Indian Continent and the Himalayas, as sketched above, might take something over a year; but it is hard to imagine a more pleasant and profitable manner of spending twelve to fifteen months.

CHAPTER IV

THE FORESTS AND THE WILD SPORTS OF INDIA

Forest area of India—Character of the forest and jungle—The sorts of big game—The wild sports—The wild goat and the wild sheep of the Himalaya—The tiger—The panther—The bear—The wild boar- and pig-sticking—Elephant-catching—The hooded cobra—The alligator

If the visitor to India desires sport he must give up his time to it, and be content with seeing what he can of the country while going to or returning from his hunting grounds. This, too, holds good whether his sojourn be in the winter or the summer, for the sports worth pursuing are very wild. Consequently, distances are great and access is difficult. So without weeks and weeks of time nothing can be done in this way.

In the Himalayan region the forest grounds

are too steep and rocky to be occupied by man; and the forests, with their denizens, continue very much as they have always been. But the shrinkage of the forests in India proper, owing to the invasion of the plough, the retreat of wild animals before the advance of man, the consequent diminution of the wild sports, are matters of common fame. Even then, however, several mountain ranges in Central, Eastern and Western India defy agricultural invaders. The Government, too, have during this generation awaked to a sense of the value of their forests, and have brought a vast area, greater than that of the British Isles, under forest conservancy, constituting thereby a marked addition to the resources of the State. This, together with a further area still in private hands, makes up an enormous field for the sportsman. Such an area still abounds in animals, some flesh-eating and ferocious, others timid and feeding on herbage, the latter being the natural food of the other. Others, again, although living on fruit and vegetables, can be very fierce if attacked. Others, again, live on fish, and can under some circumstances be dangerous.

The forests in the Himalaya consist of cone-bearing trees, of cedar, pine, fir, such also as juniper, yew, cypress, all in magnificent abundance, of some trees well known in Europe like the oak, the ilex, the birch and the plane, of trees highly ornamental, such as the rhododendron, the magnolia, and the tree-fern. The forest in India proper consists of deciduous trees, many of which, though valuable and useful in every way, are not known in Europe. Some, however, are known, like the teak, the tamarind, the ebony and the bamboo. Where the bamboos grow in quantities together they form one of the most exquisitely beautiful portions of the vegetable kingdom. Flowery shrubs, almost as large as trees, are commonly found. Some trees, through insect life, afford fine red dyes. The tall grasses, too, rise with their hairy heads waving in the breeze. The aspect of the forest is never gloomy ; though umbrageous enough, it is yet cheerful under the Indian sun,

TROPICAL FOREST, WESTERN INDIA

BAMBOO GROUPS, CENTRAL INDIA

and almost invariably gladdens the heart of the beholder. The undergrowth, though sometimes dense, is seldom rank or noxious, except, of course, in the deltaic regions. Every one likes marching in the forest districts in most seasons, save in the autumn, when the malaria rises and when the sylvan beauty becomes treacherous. To him who listens at night or in any calm noon-day hour, the infinitude of sounds, loud or low, soft or shrill, is marvellous, when nought is visible of the creatures, feathered or four-footed, big or minute, who are living in the arms, the bosom, the lap of the jungle, as their voices betray their presence.

In regard to birds, there is not much of that game in the forest. Such sport is best to be found in the marshy lakes near the great rivers, and in the highly cultivated fields. The quail-shooting in the young corn-fields of Western India is not surpassed in any country. Over many a marsh and lake the sky is at times partially darkened by the circling flights of aquatic fowl.

The deer and antelope of many species, with their pointed or bending horns and their branching antlers, are pursued, with fatigue certainly, but without danger, just as they are stalked in the British Isles. So is the bison, though under certain circumstances at close quarters his horns may be dangerous. It is, however, the spice of danger that lends interest to the wild sports. The danger may arise from the nature of the localities; it generally arises from the character of the animals.

In the higher Himalaya the pursuit of the wild goat and the wild sheep is the most arduous. The sportsman at the best has but the scantiest reward for immense exertions, with all risks from precipice, crevice and glacier, in more than Alpine altitudes. If he fails in sport he still sees mountain scenery of the most exalted character better than any one else can see it, and he communes with Nature in her most sublime mood. In the lower Himalayas, including the submontane zone called the Terai, the game is much the same as that of India proper, but with somewhat greater risk in respect of malaria.

In India the lion is rare, and when found is of no account. The king of Indian beasts is the tiger, and of all the varieties of the race the Bengal tiger has the highest repute, probably because he is the best fed, being able to prey upon cattle. Often he lurks in sub-Himalayan jungles near the river Brahmaputra. Being, like most wild beasts, a capital swimmer, he will often swim across a broad river to some small wooded island as a hiding-place or a storehouse for the bodies of the cattle he has killed. He can be surrounded here without a chance of escape, and then he will show fearful fight at the very closest quarters. The sportsman, too, must attack him without the help of elephants. This is a very fine opportunity of tiger-shooting; but the sportsmen should be first-rate hands, otherwise disaster will occur.

The tiger elsewhere, who must spend an active night in stalking the fleet and wary antelope, has a precarious livelihood, and is leaner. He is a coward before man, and will fly from a human pursuer as long as there is any chance of safety in flight. When marching in the forest one first hears the deep roar of the tiger an instinctive fear arises. But in reality all is safe; he will not come near. He would never attack a man unless he were a man-eater, and if he were, then no roar or sound would issue from him; he would steal up noiselessly like death and the grave. A tap from his velvet paw on the head of the unsuspecting man would stun the victim; some blood would be sucked from the throat, the body would be lifted up by the powerful mouth, and carried to a lair where the ghastly meal might be completed later on. The man-eater is usually one who has failed in the ordinary business of a tiger. The regular tiger is a born sportsman. Consummate in the art of stealthily pursuing his game, he is equally skilful in eluding pursuit when he is himself pursued. Still he must have his lairs, and, above all, his drinking places in the dry heat, the solitary tarn, the attenuated streamlet. The pairs of human eyes that peer about in watchfulness are at length too much for even his sagacity, and the elephants with the marksmen are upon him. He receives bullet after bullet in his body without flinching and yet goes on. Finally he feels that he can carry no more bullets or that his strength is failing—as the bullets may be causing internal hæmorrhage—or that there is some barrier-like rock, or that enemies are hemming him in. Then he resolves to retreat no further. Now are seen the amazing flexibility and elasticity of his muscular system; with his mighty bound, his bright tawny side and dark stripes, he looks like a vision as he sweeps through the air. Then, too, it is that he puts all his force into that terrible spring with which his fame has long been celebrated—right for the nearest elephant. Confident in the rifle of his rider, the noble elephant gathers up his trunk and presents his broad forehead to the tiger, like a British square receiving cavalry. If the tiger is stopped by the bullet—well. If not, then in an instant the tiger, with teeth and jaw and claws of all four feet, fastens himself on the broad flank of the elephant. I shall not follow up the crisis which ensues, and which may end in disaster or may be averted in many possible ways.

The worst of all dangers is that which often arises when the stricken tiger lies low, apparently wounded unto death. The temptation is for the hunter to approach too near and thus to come within reach. Then the dying tiger summons up his last energies to wreak revenge on his destroyer. More wounds have been inflicted on sportsmen, more gallant lives have been lost, in this stage of tiger-hunting than in any other.

For all that, the tiger is not the most dangerous animal of the jungle. The palm in that grim respect must be awarded to the panther, a sort of leopard, grey with black spots, extremely light in body, relatively to the long muscular limbs, consequently having an agility unequalled by any creature whatever. He is pursued in much the same way as the tiger, but is more courageous and readier to resist. The spring of the tiger is that of blind fury and despair directed at the nearest object without any thought. But the panther has cunning thought in his spring, and he means vengeance on his assailant. Two sportsmen might be perched up on big branches of trees by moonlight, watching a panther come to drink. Both may fire and hit. Instantly the panther will climb up one tree with amazing quickness and punish the sportsman. He will then with equal velocity ascend the other tree and deal with the man up there. Lives of men have been lost in some such way as this. In no other case is such ferocity directed with a cunning almost amounting to reason.

The bear is the most stupid animal in the forest. But the character of the she-bear with whelps is different. Maternal instinct gives her for a while an aggressive fierceness to which bearish nature is usually a stranger. But when pushed to close conflict and smarting under agony of gunshot wounds, the bear will round on his enemy. He will grapple with the muzzle of the rifle, or if he can reach the man's body then his gnawing bite is dreadful. Sometimes near a jungle path the bear lies quiet in the dusk though the wayfarer is approaching. In what may be figured as vacuity of mind, he lets the wayfarer stumble over him. Then he rises in surprise and with his long nails strikes at the man's head. I have seen a man's face scratched away—all features gone—with one stroke of the claw. The proper precaution at dusk is to sing or shout as one walks along; if there be any bear on the path he will, on hearing this, move off.

The queen sport of India is wild boar-spearing, commonly called pig-sticking. This is on horseback, and the boar often takes the hunt and the field over such a stiff country with so many blind ravines that accidents are reduced to a certainty. The Bengal boar, feeing on sugarcane illicitly consumed, is well fed and short tempered. After galloping for a bit at full speed his breath fails him, and he resolves to stop and fight. Elsewhere the boar, being less fed and in better running condition, goes further, and in some places he will give the field a long run just as a fox does in England. In all cases the mode of fighting is the same. The boar is wounded by spear after spear as the well-mounted riders come up with him. Then he suddenly stops and "squats," as the phrase goes. That is to say he turns round, sits on his hindquarters and faces the horsemen with his mighty snout armed with the protruding tusks. The next step on either side may depend on various circumstances demanding all the qualities of the best sportsman; but anyhow there is a crisis. If the boar charges, he may be stopped by the horseman's spear. If that fails, then the horse is probably lost, being ripped up by one twist or turn of the tusk. If the horseman, on rolling over, is caught by the boar, then he may be killed in the same way. But that is not likely, because the boar after ripping up the horse rushes on madly without waiting to deal with the horseman.

The killing of elephants as a high kind of sport is carried on in other countries more completely than in India. The object in India is to capture these valuable animals for service, rather than to kill them. In the central part of India I have known these fine creatures caught in this wise. A gigantic **V** is formed in the forest by rough palisades growing in strength and massiveness near the pointed end. The herd is driven by beaters into the broad end of the **V**, which operation is not difficult, as the breadth may be a mile or more. The herd moving before the beaters finds itself more and more confined at every step till the point of the **V** is reached, and its movements are fully circumscribed. Then comes the tussle for capture or escape, and the struggles can be imagined with which the hugh beasts strive to effect their freedom, but in vain, as the ropes and the lassoes are too strong.

Though venomous snakes often destroy natives in the jungle, they rarely trouble Europeans. The hooded cobra, however, in South-Western India does appear menacingly at times. I do not remember any casualty occurring, but I have myself been more than once threatened by him.

There remains a reptile not usually pursued for sport, but yet deserving of mention, and that is the snub-nosed alligator, feeding not on fish but on carrion, and quite amphibious. Along the margin of certain rivers there will be sandy slopes, often in the midst of attractive scenery. In all India there is nothing so perilous as to walk along these sands near the water's edge. There will be bits of grey rock and grey-bleached logs of wood lying about on the sand. Among them there may be lying a grey alligator, motionless and undistinguishable from a stone or a log. If the wayfarer be above the alligator, that is, on the outer side from the water, there is little danger, for the reptile when on land is wholly a coward and diffident of any movement, having only the meanest legs, and depending on his scaly tail for motion. But if the wayfarer comes between the alligator and the stream, then the reptile with his powerful tail propels himself with velocity over the few yards of sand, opens his jaws armed with long rows of teeth, and drags his victim under water.

To give an idea of the horrid quality of this alligator, I will cite a native legend regarding him—it is hardly more than a legend, based on probability, for scarcely any one could have seen such an event happen. A tiger coming to drink crawls along the sand between the alligator and the water, as I supposed the wayfarer to do. Instantly the alligator is upon the tiger's body. Did the tiger know his chance he would get one of his claws under the alligator's soft belly and rip it up with his fearfully armed paw, whereupon the reptile's grip would be relaxed. Instead of that he directs his mighty teeth and his sharp claws on the alligator's back. But all in vain, for there the alligator is protected by impenetrable scales. Still the tiger with his muscular force resists, but after a few moments he is drawn under the water by the leverage of the alligator's tail.

CHAPTER V

THE NATIONALITIES AND RELIGIONS OF INDIA

Many nationalities in India — The Hindus — Their origin—Their faith, ancient and modern—Booddhism ancient and pure, modern and debased—Effect of Western education on Hinduism—General character of the Hindu race—The aboriginal races—The Moslems; those who are of Central Asian descent, those who are descended from Indian races—The Parsees of Western India—Retrospect of native virtues.

THE land, in plain and mountain, in field and forest, in town and country, having been briefly described, it is now time to glance at the people. Although the visitor's gaze is incessantly turned in diverse directions, first to this object then to that, still he will desire to know something of the races, classes, and masses of men among whom he is moving, however rapidly.

India is well known to be the land of many

nationalities, and of many tongues, not dialects only, but written languages. The population (including British territories, the native States, and Burma) is now stated at 290 millions, and has heretofore increased fast. In the decade ending 1890 there had been an increase by natural increment of 35 millions, almost as many as the population of the British Isles: that was in ten years which had been free from famine. In the current decade famine will have checked the increase. Still, in all probability, the population will ere long amount to three hundred millions, a number nearly equal to the population of Europe.

The nationalities may be grouped under three heads: (1) Hindu; (2) Moslem; (3) Aborigines.

The Hindus now number about two hundred and twenty millions, one of the largest nationalities in the world under one Government, equal to the population of the British Isles, France, Spain, Italy, and Germany, taken together. They have all one faith, with certain variations—in other words, they all adopt one or other of the several authorised varieties of the same faith. They are all of one dark complexion, otherwise they display great varieties of physique, as might be expected, considering that they occupy more than twenty-five degrees of latitude. The one sacred and classical—though dead—language to which they all appeal is the Sanscrit. Their spoken languages are several, as follows: The Hindi (Northern India), which is the most orthodox, being the one most directly derived from the Sanscrit. Then there are the Mahratti and Guzerathi for Western India, the Bengalee, the Oorya and the Telugu for Eastern India—all of Sanscrit derivation. To these might be added the Gurmukhi of the Sikhs in the Punjab, inasmuch as the Sikh faith is not separate from Hinduism, but is only a reformed version of it. For South India, there are the Tamil or Dravidian, of *non*-Hindu origin, and the Canarese, of mixed origin, but largely Dravidian. Some of them, too, speak

Malayalam, of Malay origin, to a limited extent.

The question then arises, who are the Hindus? Well, they were men of Central Asia, of the region now occupied by Samarcand and Bokhara, who emigrated, crossed the Himalaya, and settled on the Gangetic plain called Hind—a name which afterwards gave the appellation of Indus to the river. Hence they took their name, Hindu. They had four castes—the priestly, or Brahmin; the warrior, in later ages called Rajput; the Kayasth and Vaisiya, that is, the clerkly and the trading classes. Below all these were the Sudras, or low caste. The Hindu emigrants found a considerable aboriginal population, which they gradually drove into the mountains. The aborigines who remained in the open country became merged in the Sudras. The priestly, the clerkly, and the trading classes did not intermarry with the aborigines, but the warrior class did so largely, perhaps in a loose way, the children thus born being counted as Sudras. But to this day there are classes aboriginal by the maternal side, perhaps Rajputs by the paternal, who like to call themselves Rajputs on this account, though their aspect at once betrays them.

The next question would be, what is the Hindu faith? Well, as transmitted from Central Asia to India it was a pure and simple belief in God as visible in Nature, full of moral wisdom, and embodied in the famous books known as "Vedas." Then, as the Brahmins grew in influence, it became fantastically overlaid with false philosophy and grotesque mythology, till it became not the Hindu but the Brahminical faith. As it became worse and worse during the course of centuries, there arose in Northern India (Oudh and Behar) a moral and religious reformation under a leader who took the title of Booddha (abstract wisdom) and founded Booddhism, which rose to be the State religion. So Booddhism reigned from one end of India to the other for several centuries and spread to foreign countries. Ultimately Brahminism revived, reasserted itself with force, stamped out Booddhism throughout India, restricting it to the foreign countries, where it still survives. In these countries was included Burma, which has subsequently become British and where Booddhism still prevails. In one corner of the Himalaya is Booddhism still to be found, and that is Sikkim. The restored Brahminism has now flourished for some centuries in India, and is what modern people call Hinduism.

But as already stated, modern Hinduism has several varieties, which are in this wise. There is a Triad—the creative force (Brahma), the preserving force (Vishnu), the destructive force (Siva). Brahma commands, indeed, a general reverence, but the popular worship is either for Vishnu or for Siva. But Siva has a wife named Kali, and she counts as many worshippers as he. They have their followers in all the various sections and languages of the Hindus, as already described. There is a learned class, named Pandits, who study philosophy and ethics. In dialectics they would hold their own with similar classes in any country. Besides these there will be classes of devout and well-instructed Brahmins, who throw a pious spirit into minute observances. But outside these considerable classes, the ordinary and common Hindus seem never to get beyond externals—pouring oil, burning incense, painting the forehead, preserving cows, scattering flowers, abstaining from or taking certain food at certain times ; and, above all things, bowing before the shrine and the idol. Under all circumstances their offerings and gifts for sacred purposes are probably immense. The religious demeanour of the people is mild, and fights between rival sections are almost unknown. But in and about the greater temple precincts, where many Brahmins are congregated, there is a fanaticism which might easily burst into flame. The mass of Hindus could not give any rational or connected account of their faith. They would, however, declare their belief in the potent effect of the wrath of their god or goddess, and their hope in the efficacy of propitiation.

One virtue, partly religious and partly pertaining to humane sentiments, they possess in a degree not surpassed in any country, and that is practical charity. They acknowledge and act up to the obligation of the village community to support the sick, the destitute and the aged. That which is done by the Poor-law in the British Isles is managed by voluntary effort all over India.

The Hindu faith, as above sketched, is no longer believed in by the Hindus educated on the Western model. This class, constantly growing in number and influence, and sometimes called by the name of Brahmo, generally seeks to revert to the elder faith of the Vedas already mentioned.

The Hindus generally avail themselves of the education offered by the British Government, whether Western, or Oriental, or practical, much more readily than the Moslems, and reap thereby an advantage in the race of life. But this does not affect the religious belief or practice of the masses; and the controversies that arise occasionally when young men or boys desire to embrace Christianity show how strongly and deeply Hinduism is interwoven with the national existence.

Besides the main persons in the Hindu faith, there are lesser gods, and saints and incarnations to fill the Pantheon. Of these the most important is Rama, the hero of the Hindus, as Hercules was of the Greeks. The most popular is Krishna, in the gladness of youth, exactly the Apollo of the Hindus. There are local sanctities too—the rivers Ganges, Hooghly, and Nerbudda are sacred. Many are the places of pilgrimage resorted to by immense multitudes. The most famous of these is Hardwar, at the point where the Ganges debouches from the Himalaya, and there the spectacle of the pilgrimage is most imposing. The feasts and holidays connected with religion are numerous. On these gala occasions the crowds, with their turbans, their waistbands, their scarves, in reds, in scarlets,

NATIVE FAIR ON BANK OF RIVER NERBUDDA

FESTIVAL AT GOVERDHAN, NEAR MATHRA

in oranges, in yellows, contrasting against white vests, present a brilliant display of colour and movement, surpassing the effect of a kaleidoscope, a flowery mead, a modern garden. All this, too, may be set off by flights of stone steps, by reflections in the sacred tanks, by the graceful stone carvings of the temple architecture, and by the green of the umbrageous trees, the mango, the peepul, the banyan, with all the elements of pictorial effect.

The ideas of the average Hindu regarding the future state after death have never been discovered by me. I think he expects absorption into the divine being or essence ; he does not believe in annihilation. He has much less fear of "something after death" than a Christian. Though not quite courageous in the European sense, he yet faces death with intrepidity.

There are certain characteristics common to all the sections of the great Hindu nationality. Such are the rigid adherence to custom ; the observance of caste notwithstanding modern education ; the family affection and domestic virtue ; the pity for suffering and desire to relieve it ; the profound reverence for things unseen. The people do not fully come up to what I hope is the British standard of truthfulness, integrity, fidelity and honour. Certainly they are wonderful adepts in telling a made-up tale. But the circumstances of many centuries have been cruelly against them in these respects. It would be un-Christian to pass a harsh judgment on them ; under better auspices they have improved and will yet further improve. At all times there have been among them signal instances of virtue. Personal fidelity has often been evinced by them under trial and temptation. In patient endurance under calamity they are excelled by none. Intellectually, in memory, in application, in imitative power, in imagination and speculation, they will not be surpassed anywhere. In inventive capacity, in practical application of science, in inductive thought, in the more robust qualities of the mind, they are not nearly equal to Europeans.

Physically, the Brahmins are handsome, interesting and finely shaped, in all parts of the country, though they are better looking in the north than the south. The northern Brahmins possess the traits of countenance and manner which come from purity of descent during many ages, to a degree greater, as I suppose, than any other race in the world. These fine qualities are universal among this very numerous class, though, of course, varying infinitely in degree among individuals. Otherwise there are great differences among other castes and classes. The Bengalee has more of mind than of body, is unwilling to serve in the army though most industrious in civil life; the North-West man is ever ready for military service; the Punjabi is sturdier still; the Rajput is more the child of chivalry; the Mahratta has more of the bull-dog temper and aspect; the Telugu is milder but still has martial instincts. In the southern peninsula there has been less of war and revolution, so the popular qualities are less marked.

Some barbarities which disgraced Hindu society, like widow-burning or female infanticide, have been stopped under British rule. Child marriage and the prohibition of re-marriage for widows, the seclusion of women in the upper classes, the ruinous extravagance even among the humble classes on wedding occasions, still exist, and are among those things which cannot be checked by any Government. There is something admirable about them even here, inasmuch as the generosity of a gentleman, the principle of *noblesse oblige*, is felt by all classes, even the humble. The rigorous bonds of caste show no signs of loosening for the people at large, though relaxed for individuals who cross the ocean.

The Moslems are more than fifty millions in number, the largest aggregation of adherents to Islam under any one dominion. Consequently the Empress of India is truly said to have more Moslem subjects than any Sovereign in the world. Nevertheless, the composition of this aggregate needs examination ethnologically. A portion only will be

THE GANGES AT BENARES

found to come from Central Asian stock—Persian, Arabian, Mogul, Afghan, and so forth. Consequently this portion only will have the qualities of those races—qualities which may be either valuable or dangerous according to circumstances. Again, a portion only would have the excitable fanaticism which is ever to be dreaded. Still this portion, which may be termed the Moslems proper, is quite big enough to be a great factor in the country at large, and this is the portion which might conceivably be acted upon by influences outside India. There are, indeed, many noble characters among them—brave gentlemen in every sense of the term. The remainder of the aggregate, indeed the majority, is made up of low caste Hindus, generally of pliable and pacific temper, who in former times have been converted forcibly to Islam, and who, happening to occupy fertile lands fitted for extension of agriculture, have increased and multiplied amazingly. These do not differ from Hindus except in religion, and indeed are good people of the mildest type. The

Moslems proper, of Central Asian descent, have always been among the brave soldiers of the Empire, and thriven very much in our military service. In civil capacities they were largely employed under British rule up to the present generation, outnumbering the Hindus in these departments. But in this generation the superior aptitude of the Hindus for education has given them the advantage in competition, and the Moslems have somewhat fallen behind.

It may be added that the Indian Moslems chiefly belong to the Sunni division of Islam, of which the Turkish Sultan is the head. In some parts of India the Shiah division—of which the Shah of Persia is the head—is largely represented. Conflicts between these sects have sometimes caused anxiety.

The Moslems proper are not always on good terms with the Hindus, sometimes one might apprehend that the two are very ready to fly at each other's throats. Rioting of the worst kind has arisen in this way. Anything that affects the cow may rouse the Hindus to sudden fury and frenzy. The Moslems are attacked in their mosques, and they retaliate on the temples. Then the British step in to answer for order. Not long ago a disturbance of this kind in Bombay became so bad that European artillery had to be called in to threaten to sweep the streets.

The term Aborigines is commonly applied to certain tribes inhabiting the hilly parts of the continent, and indeed they are aboriginal as compared with the Hindus. But the prehistoric remains scattered over India, in common with other countries, show that there must have been some still older nationality of whom we have no trace save these silent monuments. Apart from this antiquarian question, the aborigines of to-day, as popularly known, are the descendants of the aborigines who were not absorbed into the low caste Hindus, as already explained, or who have not been subsequently converted to Hinduism by the proselytising influences ever at work. These aborigines are represented by tribes dwelling in the hills to the west and east of Bengal, and along the eastern coast of India, that is, the coast of the Bay of Bengal, and in the central mountain ranges, which run athwart the country from east to west, and form the dorsal ridge of the continent. Some few are found in the Nilgherry mountains in the south-west corner of India. The tribes are known as Gonds, Santhals, Khassias, and others. Inside their own hills they are good cultivators, foresters, sportsmen. In fighting wild beasts their courage is superb. Outside their own hills they have generally been of no account. In some places they have signalised themselves by works of irrigation. In recent years they have been largely employed in European tea gardens among the lower Himalayas, and in Assam valleys not far from the Brahmaputra. They have dialects but scarcely a written language, though their dialects may have been reduced to writing by others. Some of them had horrid rites which were stopped by the British rule. They worship the unknown god, they affix reverential marks to stocks and stones. They

DWELLING OF ABORIGINES IN THE NILGHERRY HILLS

have happily proved amenable to Christian influences. Missionary effort has proved successful among them, and may yet find a further field, as their number amounts to many millions of souls.

Outside all these nationalities are the Parsees, descendants of Persian fire-worshippers, who would not bow the knee to the Prophet of Arabia. Their story is romantically told in Moore's "Lalla Rookh." Some centuries ago they took refuge on the western coast of India, just above Bombay. They are, though limited in numbers, some of the most influential, capable and wealthy citizens of Western India.

Respecting the people of India as a whole, those who have known them well, and who, after separation from them, look back upon their character, will recall very much that is admirable, commendable and loveable in them, despite all admitted faults. The idea entertained by some that they know not gratitude is fallacious. To such an one I would reply —govern them well, guard their interests, relieve their sufferings, save their lives, raise their status and condition, let them see that you are really labouring on their behalf, and you will find gratitude in abundance.

Even so brief a summary as this cannot be concluded without some tribute being paid to the natural picturesqueness of the people. As a rule, they are by nature artistic, following art principles almost unconsciously. They have an innate taste and are gifted with a very fine eye for colour. Wherever they abide their surroundings become picturesque. They could not describe their feeling for, nor define their ideas of, art; but they are ever showing it in all their ways and deeds. Every commanding or striking situation throughout the continent and the peninsula has been occupied by a temple or a shrine or a mosque. Their fine perception is ever shown in the selection of sites for their structures. On holidays, always connected with religious observance, the gaily dressed crowds, the swarthy faces, hands, and feet, are set off by white garments decorated with cloths and scarves of bright colours in the sunshine. These moving masses make pictures with a background of umbrageous trees or temple achitecture or sacred tanks. Again there is the floral display, with abundance rather than with refinement of floriculture, while the sacred bulls are pushing their way through the crowd. The bathing in the Ganges, when crowds rush down the flights of steps to the sacred water, presents a strangely animated spectacle, especially by moonlight. The landing-places on the river-bank where the dead are burned, and where smoke and flame ceaselessly ascend, present a scene characteristic though melancholy. At places of pilgrimage, where multitudes are for a time dwelling in booths and small tents arranged regularly in streets and squares, there is a little sea of canvas spread out. A circle of village elders in council, seated on the ground under the branches of a great banyan fig-tree, seems like a remnant of patriarchal times. On special occasions the towers with coronetted finials, the cupolas, the architectural outlines of the temples, are tastefully and gracefully illuminated by a people who are born masters of this art. When any person in authority approaches a town or village, the natives come out to meet him with innate courtesy, bearing not presents of any value but offerings of fruit and the like, investing the little scene with a picturesqueness peculiar to the country. The Hindu generally is not equestrian in these days. But the Moslems often appear in cavalcades with arms, trappings, and the like. Wondrous sights are often beheld on the water also in North-eastern India where the rivers are broad. The build, the rigging, the equipment of the boats, ever varying in structure according to the current of the streams, afford endless material for the artistic pencil. The swelling white sails strike the eye as they pass under dense and rich green masses of bamboos and other jungle on the river-bank. The floating cities, where boats are moored amid stream for weeks together in long lines like streets, are truly wondrous.

CHAPTER VI

THE NATIVE PRINCES OF INDIA

Importance and condition of the Native States—Their position in the Empire—States in the Himalaya, Nepaul, Jammu—Cashmere and Sikkim—The Protected Sikh States—Chivalry of Rajputana—Mahratta States of Sindhia and Holkar—The Nizam of the Deccan—The Mountain States of the South-western Peninsula—Mysore and Travancore—The Imperial troops of the Native States.

THE native Princes of India are numerous, some hundreds in number, ruling in a sovereign capacity about 500,000 square miles, an area as large as that of some among the European Great Powers, and some sixty to sixty-five millions of people. They are all under the suzerainty of the British Crown. Although they are, in a certain sense, equal in the common quality of sovereignty, they are of many degrees, from the prince with a kingdom as large, say, as one of the kingdoms of Germany, down to the lesser chief, who from a height could look all round his little dominion, and so be monarch of all he surveys. Thus by gradation they are the allies, or the feudatories, or the vassals, or the lieges of the British Empire. As the history of their relations with the British Government has been diverse, so the control or supervision varies both in kind and degree. But some sort of control is exercised over them all more or less. In the event of any Imperial question arising this control would grow into absolute authority. On the other hand, within their territories, they have civil autonomy. On the whole, their case resembles that of feudal chivalry in Europe, and for European analogy we may look to the States that make up the German Empire.

They may within this generation become potent factors for good in the Indian Empire. Thirty or forty years ago there was among them a dread of absorption into the British territories. From that apprehension they have long been freed. They have received the most practical assurance in a hundred ways that the succession to their heritages is to be preserved by direct lineage if possible, if not, by adoption. They feel themselves to be a cherished part of the Empire. When the Prince of Wales visited India, and afterwards when the Queen was proclaimed Empress, these native princes participated in the associations and traditions that cluster round the British crown and throne. This royal and feudal class, scattered all over India, appreciate the advantages of their position, with its entire security, and with an immunity greater than that which they ever enjoyed under native suzerains or emperors. They look up to the Queen Empress as their supreme head, puissant, gracious, and beneficent. They gladly accept the protecting ægis, they hope it may last for ever, and they would not abide the thought of a revolution. Here, then, is a backbone of conservative force in the Empire.

The native States now most interesting in English eyes are the two in the Himalaya, namely Nepaul and Jammu-Cashmere. They comprise some of the grandest scenery on earth. One of them has inherent might of a striking character. The other has a political situation of growing importance.

In some respects Nepaul is the most potent native State in the Indian Empire, and over it there is less of British control than over any other. It is guarded by mountains hard to cross, access to it by Europeans is jealously restricted, and it is less visited by the outside world than any other native State. The interest and importance attaching to it arises from the martial qualities of its people—the Gorkhas. It allows these fighting men to enlist largely in the British service, and the world sees how well they behave in battle. Speculative politicians well know that if anything had happened, or were ever to happen, fatal to British rule, there would have been, or would be, a Gorkha dynasty in North Eastern India. The Nepaul valley girdled with hills is very fine indeed, but not all comparable to Cashmere, though the snow-clad peaks of the Nepaulese mountains are of a very high rank. It has one Booddhist pagoda of extreme beauty. Climbing up a flight of steps, darkly shaded and of irksome length, the spectator perceives the gilded pinnacle far above him piercing the blue sky. The gem, however, is a great Hindu temple (at Patun), which with the adjuncts constitutes a glorious and unique specimen of Oriental architecture. The fundamental ideas are Indian, but the roofs, the finials, and everything that makes up the outline against the sky, are of Chinese conception, and in fantastic style. The whole structure is bright and airy, replete with imagination, yet massive and imposing. The materials, the brickwork, pink enamelled, the teak wood-carving, the stamped brass, the gilded copper, the unprotected copper turning emerald in colour, the grey limestone images of gigantic size, produce a combination gorgeous and impressive. Long shadows are flung across the paved roadway, which will be crowded with soldiers in red uniform, by hillmen and women in parti-coloured vestments, and with saffron-coloured umbrellas. Behind all this are the blue mountains surmounted by peaks of everlasting snow. This is certainly one of the finest scenes in the Indian Empire.

The State of Jammu-Cashmere is in the western Himalaya overlooking the Panjab. Take Cashmere all in all, with its complete circle of snow-capped mountains, its view of the main Himalayan range, its cedar forests, its winding river and pellucid lake, its antiquities and ruins, both Hindu and Moslem, its domestic architecture, its exquisite fabrics, its picturesque population, its lovely climate for half the year, it is probably the most beautiful place on earth. The Italian lakes are the only places that could be compared with it; and I believe that it is superior even to them. The founder of the Jammu State, with the favour of the British Government, was Golab Sing, half a century ago, in graceful dignity the finest native Prince in Northern India. Later on, I well remember, when John

Lawrence visited him at Jammu, how he came out with his followers on elephants right into the water of the river flowing underneath the palace-fortress, as we were riding with the stream almost up to our saddle girths. How picturesque was the line of caparisoned elephants amid-stream underneath the frowning rocky heights. Within the last few years the outlying mountain valleys of Cashmere extend up to the Pamir region which has been partitioned between England and Russia. These valleys, embosomed amidst the loftiest groups of the snow-clad Himalaya, thus become the outworks of the British Empire in this quarter. It was partly on this account that the famous district of Chitral was subdued and has been retained.

There is yet one more smaller State in the Eastern Himalaya, namely Sikkim, within sight of the well-known British station of Darjeeling, and with scenery of unsurpassed magnificence. It extends right up to Tibet. The frontier in that quarter—a meeting point of the British and Chinese Empires—is marked by a series of lovely lakes, having an average altitude of 13,000 feet above sea level. Yet another feature in Sikkim consists of its monasteries, belonging to what may be called the debased Booddhism. The umbrella-shaped roofs, the mushroom-like formations, the massive masonry, sometimes red stained, the grotesque frescoes, the coloured wood carvings, make the structures look weird amidst the thick forests with the everlasting snows overhead. In the chapels, with richly painted walls and ceilings, the monks, in their maroon-coloured vestments and saffron silks, sing their service with an accompaniment of long brass trumpets, while the image of Booddha with ineffable calm looks down on the scene, which is one of the most characteristic to be seen in the whole Himalaya.

At the base of the western Himalaya is a group of Protected Sikh native States, notable for their loyalty during the crisis of the Mutinies in 1857. On the Sutlej, not far

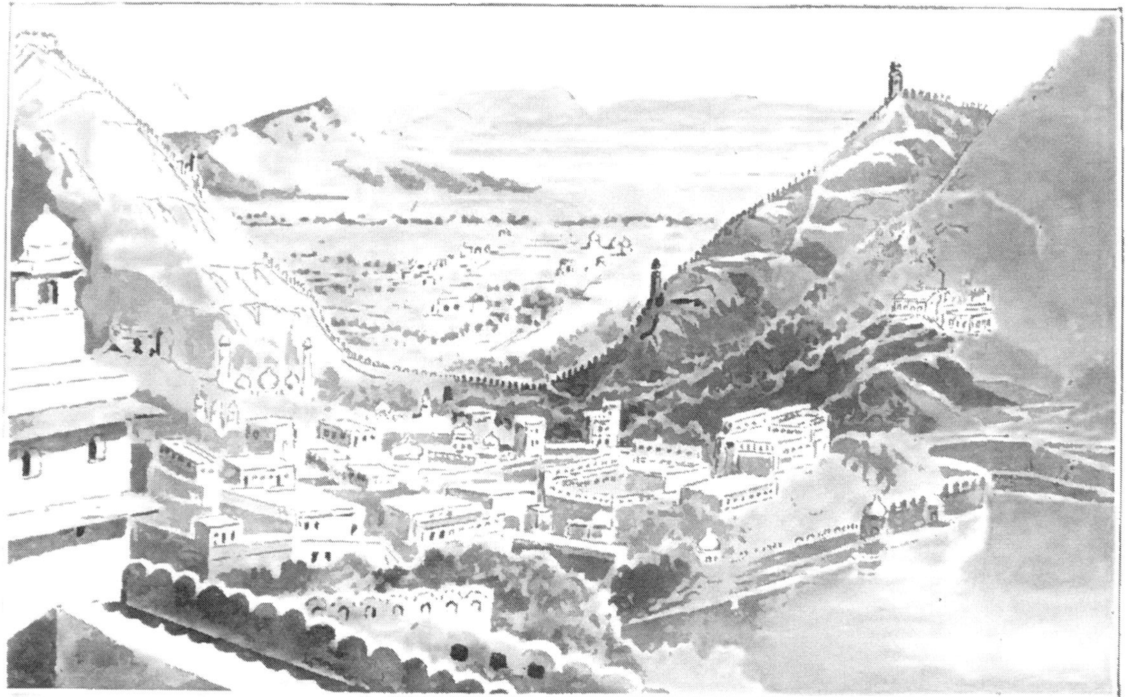

OLD AMBAIR, NEAR JYEPORE

off, is the Prince of Kapoorthalla, also Sikh, whose troops have recently shared with our own the deadly perils of the Trans-Indus frontier. These several courts should be visited by those who would study the aspect of the stalwart Sikhs of grenadier stature.

Next we approach the great cluster of native States to the south of the upper Gangetic valley, that is, just below Delhi and Agra, which has the generic name of Rajputana, the country of Rajputs. The Princes are the living active representatives of the original caste of Hindu warriors, as already explained. The two principal States of this most interesting group—Oodeypore and Jyepore—have been mentioned also, and need not be adverted to further. As they abut, with their mountains and their sandy desert tracts, on the fertile plains of the Jamna and the Ganges, they were formidable to the Moslem invaders. Accordingly Akber the Great paid courtly attention to them when he founded the Mogul Empire, with its imperial headquarters at

Agra. Being himself a freethinker, though brought up rigorously in the faith of Islam, he did not hesitate to propose matrimonial alliances with the princely Rajput families, and his successors naturally did the same, having indeed an infusion of Hindu blood in their veins. That these royal Hindu houses should have agreed to such alliances may seem almost incredibly strange to those who know the force of Hindu caste and faith. Great, however, was Diana of the political forces. These Rajput brides of Moslem conquerors were treated with the loftiest consideration, which indeed kept Rajputana in loyal alliance with the Mogul Empire. They were doubtless permitted to lead their Hindu lives in the Moslem zenana. Their architectural surroundings were actually preserved, so that the early associations of their childhood might not be broken in their married homes. For them were built the Moslem palaces near Agra, of red sandstone. For them were summer-houses planted on the Lake of Cashmere, with the black marble of

GWALIOR CITADEL ROCK

Central Asia. In these structures the style was based on the severe Moslem principles, but the adornment, carving, and sculpture were in the rich and fantastic manner of the Hindus, with a wondrous but still beauteous combination. He who would comprehend Rajputana aright must recall the old ideas of European chivalry and romance. This chain of sentiment and this train of thought survive and prevail among the Rajputs. The feudal notions, with the inward devotion and loyalty to ideal standards, the outward grace in feature, stature, aspect and demeanour, the grand externals in armour, in costume, in equipage—in paraphernalia generally—are still to be found better than anywhere else in India among these Rajput Princes who claim to be descended from the sun and moon.

The Mahratta States of Central India adjacent to Rajputana—namely, Sindhia at Gwalior, and Holkar at Indore, have already been mentioned. To these the State of the Gaikwar of Baroda, below the mountains and on the sea coast, may be added. Their courts will have less of nobility, of elegance and refined dignity than those just alluded to. They will, however, be found to have something of solid grandeur. Their architectural surroundings are not fine. Unfortunately, the two splendid monuments which the Mahratta nationality possessed, namely, the carved teakwood palaces of Nagpore and Poona—among the finest things of their kind in any country—have been destroyed by fire within this generation.

In the south, or Deccan, the Moslem State is that of the Nizam of Hyderabad—the premier Prince of India. When the Mogul Empire destroyed the five Moslem kingdoms which had long existed in the Deccan—each of which has left remains and monuments, often of exquisite beauty and interest—a Mogul Viceroy was established representing in the Deccan the Mogul Emperor, and styled the Nizam. These Viceroys, or Nizams, had become hereditary and independent by the time that the British power appeared on the horizon. In the wars that followed they

VIEW OF HYDERABAD, DECCAN

became the allies of the British Government represented by the East India Company. And although the Nizam of to-day depends on the British power for support, he would claim to be considered as an ally rather than a feudatory. Placed in the midst of a Hindu population, Telugu and Mahratta, the Nizams have found it difficult to provide enough of Moslem force. So they have from time to time called in the aid of martial Arabs from Arabia. These men have on some occasions become like the Pretorian Guards or the Janissaries of old. Even now their presence is a sort of embarrassment. On parades of the multifarious army of the Nizam's troops, their rough, stern features, their square-built frames, dark brown skins and snow white garments, with their muskets, pouches and daggers, form a significant contrast to the gay costumes, the burnished armour, the decorated trappings, the olive complexions, and the handsome features of the Deccan soldiery.

Further to the south, on the lofty plateaux

of the Western Ghaut Mountains, is the Hindu State of Mysore, restored by the British after the conquest and death of the Moslem Tippoo Sultan. The palace is remarkable for its hall of audience, with its noble perspective of arches and pillars. At the southern extremity of the range is the Hindu State of Travancore amidst vegetation and scenery of a tropical character.

The native Princes, whose personality and individuality have been conspicuous during the stirring events of this generation, and whose portraiture might well be rendered by word-painting, have passed away. The comparative quiet of the present time has hardly as yet given their successors a chance of winning a personal position. Many of them have been educated under British auspices, and nearly all of them are ruling their territories in harmony with the just, enlightened, and progressive spirit of the time. In many native States, indeed, the administration has advanced nearly as fast as in the British territories.

Apart from the Prince himself in a native

State, the heritage of ancient renown, the centre of popular veneration, the stately surroundings, still remain. Their troops, as they become better disciplined and organised, in part, at least, are not quite so picturesquely characteristic as they once were, especially when they adopt or imitate the British uniforms. The native Princes are indeed proud to improve and render effective the best portion of their troops for the purposes of the Indian Empire. The number of these effective troops in all the native States is not less than 22,000. Bodies of such troops have been, and are, employed on war service with British troops, forming an appreciable addition to our military strength, and producing a moral effect on the whole country. Besides these there are troops in great numbers but in a less organised condition. Their Oriental array, though loose, would be picturesque in appearance.

On all public occasions the court of a native Prince lacks that fairest of ornaments which European courts always possess and display. There are never any native Princesses to be seen. In one case, indeed, the Begum, or ruling Princess, of Bhopal did thus appear in the same manner as that of a Prince. When she received British Knighthood I myself had, as a brother knight, to escort her Highness up to the Viceregal daïs. But this is an exceptional if not a solitary instance. Otherwise I never saw the faces of native Princesses, though I have often heard their voices from behind the embroidered curtains during official interviews. But although the Princesses have been secluded and curtained off, they have frequently, perhaps generally, exercised influence in the affairs of their States and their families. Indeed the parts they have played in history despite all disadvantages would well deserve a separate article, and their story would redound to the credit of womanhood.

The pomp and circumstance of the native courts and camps are so remarkable that this subject must be reserved for the next chapter.

CHAPTER VII

THE COURTS AND CAMPS OF THE NATIVE PRINCES

Characteristic ceremonies at the Courts of Native Princes—A State procession—Precincts of the Palace—Reception by the Prince—Aspect of Native nobles—Pyrotechnic displays—Various festivities—Royal sports and battue in the forest—Sylvan picturesqueness—Hunting deer with cheetas.

THE *entourage*, the attendant circumstances of native Princes—always of a dramatic character, like a *mise-en-scène*—vary infinitely according to the scenery and the climate of the territory. For it must never be forgotten that the Princes are scattered over several climes and many degrees of latitude and longitude. But in many, perhaps in most cases, there will be a generic resemblance. The best, indeed the only way of depicting and portraying that, is to take an imaginary example in this wise.

A traveller should not leave India without seeing, if he possibly can, one or more of the native Princes at home, amidst the court, the state, the pomp. Let us suppose that he has made friends with the British Resident at one of these courts, and is paying a visit about the time of some ceremonial occasion relating to business with the British Government, or some festive occasion relating to the family of the Prince, and that he accompanies the Resident on the official visit.

The start would be made from the Residency in a procession—say, first, of elephants. Now an elephant, when unclad and unadorned, is an unwieldy and clumsy-looking beast. But when he is gorgeously caparisoned, has a howdah, or ornamental wooden tower, on his back, filled with richly dressed men, has another gaily clad man with an iron prong seated on his neck, and moves along with his big ears swinging to and fro like the leaves of a gigantic tree, with his sinuous trunk and his shambling gait, he somehow represents the very poetry of elephantine motion. When, say, fifty, perhaps even a hundred, of these creatures are arranged together in a long line of four abreast outside the town, and two abreast after entering the streets, the spectacle, as a combination of nature and of art, is one of unrivalled magnificence. Alongside of the procession will be lines of cavalry, horses gaily caparisoned, with cavaliers brilliant in arms, armour and equipment. The smart, nimble ambling of the horses affords a capital contrast to the wavy, ponderous, swaying movements of the elephants. The effect is that of yachts and small craft alongside of ironclads in the gala brightness of a naval review. There may be also a set of camels not so numerous, still, so far as they go, highly picturesque. The camels by themselves are far from attractive, but with their tasselled headgear, their saddles and crimson saddle-cloths, and with their riders in uniform, they become effective objects in the scenic combination. Such a procession, diversified by standards borne aloft on tall staves with the sheen of silk waving in the gentle breeze, has artistically more of the *gusto grande* than anything of the kind to be seen in Europe. So the vast *cortége* wends its way through streets, the housetops and the carved projecting balconies being crowded with groups of spectators, each group with the parti-coloured costumes looking like a tulip bed. So it nears the palace, and then the way is lined by troops, horse and foot. There is always something formal—perhaps unavoidably inartistic—about Western uniforms. Not so, however, with the martial garbs of the East. They vary with each body of men: the massive turban will be succeeded by the sharp pointed helmet, the breastplate by some rich coloured stuffs, the firelock and the short sword by the spear, the shield and the scimitar. In all cases there will be the waistband and girdle loaded with daggers. As each body presents arms one after another, the changes in the glint, the flash, the shimmer of the steel present endless variety,

SUMMER-HOUSE AT DEEG, NEAR BHURTPORE

GATEWAY OF A NATIVE PALACE

like a kaleidoscope. The National Anthem is rendered by band after band, with many faults of harmony and melody, as might be expected. As the precincts of the Palace are reached, the military give place to the civil establishments and to the servitors of the court. Line after line will appear of men bearing maces studded with bright metals, carrying flags worked with many devices, holding aloft spears with fringes and tassels, sportively brandishing burnished knives. At length the procession halts and wheels round with impressive effect, the military and civil establishments forming a gorgeous background.

So the visitor passes along the vestibules to the hall of audience, through ranks of nobles and chiefs in full dress: with turbans, embroidered vests, robes touching the ground, massive girdles, slippers finely worked. These costumes, though gorgeous, are yet harmonious in colour with artistic quality. Then jewels begin to appear. In one case the frontage of a turbaned head will sparkle with diamonds massed together in rich profusion. In another the swarthy neck will be encircled with the deep hues of the ruby and the emerald. In another there will be a breastplate resplendent with the sapphire and the onyx. In another the muscular arm will be clasped by armlets shining with the softer and paler light of pearls. In another there will be a waistband heavy laden with well-polished poignards, or with daggers velvet-sheathed and hilts embossed with jewels. The slippers peeping out from beneath the ornamental hems of the robes make as yet a pictorial finish to the costumes ; they should be looked at now, for they will presently disappear in the presence of royalty.

The figures are generally tall and well-proportioned, and the dress makes them seem taller. The countenances should be studied so far as may be possible in the few glances that are permissible. Their passing salutations and their bows are elaborately formal indeed, yet easy, graceful, flexible, and devoid of stiffness, just as if the men and their ancestors had been to the manner born, and as if they had never done anything else from their childhood onwards. The faces, too, are noble, the regular features often aquiline, the cheek bone not prominent but rather subdued, the hazel eyes full of expression, the hair of the head entirely hidden, but the trimmed and pointed moustache and long black beards set off the many hues of the dress. At the last some two or three personages will appear of yet higher rank, still more bedizened and jewelled, still more stately in their courtesy. These will be some near relations of the Prince. The attitude of all wil indicate a cordiality in the welcome they offer, and so the threshold of the audience chamber is reached.

The Prince's reception chamber may have a ceiling with massive teakwood beams and rafters, or a concave roof with a long vista of arches; in either case there will be spacious verandahs like aisles. He himself will be seated either on a raised daïs of painted wood, with cushions of glistening silk, or on a throne with gilded canopies. In either case there will be attendants waving fans of feathers or of horsehair with gilded handles to brush off imaginary flies, this ceremony being the special symbol of sovereignty. As the Resident in his uniform, his staff, and the guests approach they will be seated on chairs, and the native company already mentioned will seat themselves rapidly all around on carpets of fine texture and pattern. The latter will now be barefooted, the gilded slippers having been scrupulously left on the threshold of the chamber. Behind these figures seated on the ground, there will be massed the attendants already mentioned, now standing in groups. The whole company of all ranks have their eyes bent on the Prince with superstitious veneration perhaps, but with fervid loyalty and glowing zeal. The rays of the declining sun light up a scene sombre indeed but replete with scenic effect. Close to the Prince will be the Vizier and the chief officers of the realm, powerful

Ministers perhaps, but at this moment bending in meek submission before their master. The manner of the Prince will differ from that of the nobles already mentioned. It will evince a studied politeness indeed, but will be more distant, and will indicate a sort of self-consciousness arising from the memories of ancient pedigree and from the life-long habit of receiving reverence. The conversation will be of a formal character between the Prince and the Resident; but even then each will learn something of the other's disposition by interchanging glances and by some words dropped as if by chance amidst the formalities. Perhaps some Oriental music, with a dance called Nauch, may form a brief interlude. Stringed instruments will be played in a manner like that of the Hungarian music in Europe — airs tuneful though somewhat monotonous, and waving like the wind upon the Æolian harp. The women dancers will be robed in brilliant gauze down to the ankles; they will often sing as they dance; their movements will be measured and graceful, representing the poetry of quiet motion. Or there may be a barbaric dance with masques, one man disguised as a bear, one as a wolf, one as a monkey, and so forth; the movements being, of course, utterly grotesque.

Perhaps, too, if the occasion be one relating to the family of the Prince, there may be a presentation of gifts on ornamental trays: one tray with shawls, silks, brocade, another with rich stuffs, locally made, another with sandal-wood or satin-wood inlaid with horn and ivory, another with copper or iron exquisitely enamelled or inlaid with gold and silver, and so forth. These the Resident will accept officially, but not personally. It is a matter of courtly business; and he will send return presents as equivalents from the treasury of his Residency.

Then the Prince will call for the essence of roses with the green leaf of the betel nut, and that will be the signal for the rising of the assembly. After the strained attention, the intense curiosity, the anxiety to miss naught worth seeing, there will be momentarily a sense of relief.

In the twilight after sundown, it will be possible to see something of the palatial courtyards, the evergreens, the pomegranates, the myrtles, the orange trees, the fountains and glittering jets, the lofty walls, the lattices and trellised windows of the zenana, or women's apartments, the lofty cone of the palace temple surmounting the whole. The stables may be visited, but they will hardly impress the European visitor accustomed to the arrangements of England. So may the elephant stables, only these structures are not comparable to those which must have existed in former ages, as shown by the ruined masonry of the elephant stables to be seen in some places. The menagerie and its inmates, the tiger, the bear, the rhinoceros, the hyæna, will be in a zoological garden on a small scale. If there should be a so-called fight in an arena between wild animals, it will be an amusing affair, though somewhat clumsy, and without any serious intent on the part of either combatant. If there be an aviary that will be a rare sight, with the plumage and the varied characteristics of the birds, flying, hopping and stalking about, as if to the music of the twittering choir. Pets, too, there will be, with their pretty ways—every kind of small animal, except dogs.

Such diversions, however, are only by way of preparing for the entertainment of the evening. Torches will by this time have been lighted to guide the visitors towards some elevated terrace amidst multitudes who are by this time flitting about, the air being full of that resonance which comes from innumerable voices in laughter and joyousness. The terrace will overlook an artificial lake environed by groves of palms which cast dark reflections on the water. The darkness of these reflections will be broken by the long lines of illumination marking the margin of the lake, each lamp being doubled by its image on the water as on a mirror. Every curve in the form of the lake, every line of terrace, perhaps even the architectural details of the palace, will be picked out by lines of light. Then the fireworks will begin. Fountains with jets of golden light, mimic fortresses blazing with broadsides of fire, balls and globes of light, red, blue and green, springing into the air, rockets piercing the sky and then dropping rain of sapphire, of ruby, of emerald, of opal; and the whole display, fountains, fortress, globes and balls, rockets and rain, being so arranged as to be reflected on the lake. This duplication of effect has evidently been calculated upon beforehand. The night is advancing before the entertainment is over, and the visitor remounts his elephant amidst the sounds of the National Anthem, and returns home with a hundred images dancing about his brain. But his guiding thought will be this, that he has just moved among a people who have the dramatic instinct and an eye for effect, or for pictorial combination, not surpassed and rarely equalled by any race on earth.

Or let us take another scene and suppose that a royal hunt or battue has been appointed.

No stiff sport such as that described in a previous Chapter is to be expected, still there will be some sport of a mild type, and sights picturesque or characteristic will be met with. The road to the covert will be gay, without any regular cavalcade, but with the footrunners, and with the horsemen ambling about in the loosest order amidst the trees, the crops, the lanes. The visitors will probably be on elephants. Some amusement on the way will be provided by hawks and falcons being let loose to catch birds, and so forth. The picturesqueness increases as the motley company approaches the forest. The horsemen and footmen, all more or less brightly clad, popping, so to speak, in and out of the tall reeds and grasses, lend animation to the green of the vegetation and to the sylvan landscape. So the forest is reached, with the umbrageous trees of kinds not known in northern climes, their branches spreading widely, often environed a dense undergrowth. Then the attendant horse and foot retire. The visitor mounts a tree and is seated in a rude structure called a *machan*, which may be described as a settee with protecting sides, almost like a box, made of cane, of twigs, and the like. He fixes his gaze on the jungle, listening for a rustle in the thicket. From his vantage point amidst the foliage he is supposed to shoot the game which is beaten up towards him. Soon he will hear the voices of the beaters in the distant jungle. The big fierce game and the carnivoræ will never be encountered by him in this way, but the wild pig will come rushing past, the antelope will be fleeting by, and so he will get many a snap shot. The larger deer, with their broad flanks and lumbering gait, will afford him a far easier mark.

Or, after dismissing all miscellaneous attendants and proceeding with a few skilled persons towards the green standing crops, he may see a very curious sight, only to be had in the camp of a native Prince. In these crops deer are feeding unconcernedly. Amidst the fields are narrow roadways, along which small covered carts drawn by bullocks are constantly moving on the ordinary business of agriculture. The deer do not mind these at all, believing them to be what indeed they generally are—quite harmless. But this time one of them carries a deadly freight, blindfolded and carefully covered so that no scent may escape and give warning. This freight is a cheeta, a leopard with teeth and jaws, body and limbs of the feline order, but with paws like those of a wolf, and without retractile claws. When the cart comes within striking distance of the unsuspecting deer, the cheeta is suddenly brought out, the bandage is withdrawn from his eyes, and he beholds his prey. Instantly he goes for the deer in leaps and bounds; he knows not how to run. The deer speeds away, winged with the fleetness of agonised terror. If the cheeta be not on him within a few seconds, the game is up, the victim is saved. But each mighty bound of the cheeta is equal to a dozen strides of the frightened deer, and so in the twinkling of an eye the teeth of the pursuer may be fleshed in the hind quarters of the prey, and a cry piteous to hear issues from the dying creature. The incredible agility of the cheeta makes him seem to be flying in the air, as his feet can scarcely be seen to touch the earth at each bound.

CHAPTER VIII

THE FRONTIERS OF INDIA

Natural and geographical bounds of India—The sea around the peninsula—Vast frontier line of the Continent—On the east side towards Burma—On the north side in the Himalaya—On the north-western side by Peshawur and the Khyber—On the lower half of the same side by the Bolan Pass and Quetta—The Burmese frontier towards China—Towards Siam and French territory—Russia and France as neighbours of the Indian Empire.

FROM the consideration of the Land and the People we naturally pass on to the Government and Administration of the Indian Empire. An essential preliminary to that is a due mention of the frontiers. These include an external policy which affects the management of affairs in the interior of the country.

In several quarters the frontiers of India are

guarded by what is for Britain "the inviolable sea." In others they are fortified by Nature on a tremendous scale. But in one quarter they demand defensive arrangements of the most direct character. In another quarter they require indirect action; but such action, though intermediate, needs the consciousness that there is absolute force in the background.

The peninsula and the lower part of the continent of India are bounded by the sea, and that is for Britain the best possible frontier, requiring no further remark. For the upper and broader part of the continent there are land frontiers indeed. But the access to this part from the south on either side, east and west, is from the sea by the naval harbours of Calcutta and Kurrachee, which form the bases of British power and thus afford priceless advantages. The land frontiers, however, not south, but east, north and west, demand a few moments of consideration.

These land frontiers are of enormous length.

Let the reader cast his glance over any map, from Kurrachee, near the mouth of the Indus, then northwards along the hill ranges to a point above Peshawar—then, turning eastwards, along the southern face of the entire Himalaya to Assam—next, southwards by the deltaic region to the Ganges and the Brahmaputra, past the mouth of the Megna on to Chittagong on the Bay of Bengal, and he will have traversed in imagination several thousands of miles of land frontier. Then arise the Imperial questions: how is this enormously long frontier protected?—how much has Nature done for us?—how much remains for us to do by military art and by political arrangement? I will try to answer these questions briefly.

In the first place, Nature has done very much for us. On the eastern side there are extensive hill ranges, not lofty, but in most parts covered with well-nigh impenetrable jungle, and resting partly on Upper Burma, which has now become a great outwork of the Indian Empire. In the north-east corner the

SIKKIM-TIBET BORDER

mountains grow steeper and loftier, and the country is still more impassable. It is a no-man's-land, hardly explored ; it belongs to the Chinese Emperor if to anybody. On the great northern Himalaya line the geography and orography are more imposing than anywhere else in the world. On the northern face of this, the mightiest of mountain ranges, there is a dividing, a water-parting group of mountains. On the eastern side of the group there rises the Brahmaputra, which, after running a trans-Himalayan course eastwards for many hundred miles in Tibetan regions, suddenly turns south and bursts into India through the southern range of the Himalaya at the eastern extremity of Assam. In this quarter, beyond Sikkim, is Tibet, the most elevated plateau in the world, and really a province of the Chinese Empire. It is very thinly inhabited, and could hardly be traversed in force by any enemy of ours. On the western side of the group above mentioned there rises the Indus, which, after rushing for many hundreds of miles through deep rifts in the Himalaya, breaks into India near Attock, opposite Peshawar. Thus, with the most enormous upheavals, rifts and precipices on the whole surface of the globe, Nature herself proudly answers for the defence of the Indian Empire on the northern side. Few questions arise there except those relating to the north-western corner, as will be immediately seen.

It is on the north-western and western side that matters exist of the greatest import to the safety of the Indian Empire. There is no need to disguise the fact that these considerations relate solely to the position of Russia in Central Asia. This frontier line of ours runs mainly alongside of Afghanistan, which is virtually in alliance with us, and, figuratively, a great quickset hedge of thorns between India and the Asiatic dominions of Russia.

First let us take the north-western corner, just beyond Cashmere, that abuts on the elevated steppes of the Pamirs, a region termed by the Moslems "the roof of the

PESHAWAR AND THE KHYBER

world." This region has recently been divided between England and Russia, and it is hoped, though we can hardly feel more than hope, that the arrangement may secure our frontier in that quarter. But all this has drawn us into closer relations than formerly with many hill tribes. It was really for the sake of these, that the advance to Chitral was undertaken in 1895, and that this outpost, with the road leading thereto, is rightly retained by us.

Next let us consider the north-western section, which relates to Peshawar and to the Khyber Pass. This has been the theatre of the recent fighting already mentioned in the introductory chapter. When Alexander the Great invaded India he entered this way—that is, by northern Afghanistan, and after him several Asiatic conquerors have done the same. Possibly Russia might, under certain circumstances, try to do this also. But probably she would not ; at all events, she would have to make the attempt under such disadvantages as would be tantamount to her delivering herself into our hands. Some would say that by such conduct she would, as the phrase goes, be giving herself away. Hence it is inferred that she would be too sagacious to commit such a mistake. But she might probably make a diversion towards Caubul, the capital of our ally; and the Khyber Pass is the route to that city from our base at Peshawar. Therefore we should be in a position to be in command of that pass and other passes subsidiary to it or leading in the same direction. To all this is added the control of the Goomul Pass leading from the mid Indus valley, to Southern India and to Candahar. This matter is at the bottom of all the uprisings of the tribes and of the warlike conflicts of which the world has been following the course. The tribes, however, who have been recently contending with us, are not Afghans, nor Afghan subjects at all; indeed, they would energetically denounce the idea of Afghan sovereignty. They occupy a very long and narrow belt of mountain territory between the Indus basin and

Afghanistan, and thus they are our frontier neighbours, conterminous with us along our north-western and western boundary for many hundreds of miles. Though acknowledged on all hands as independent, they have been in the closest relations with us for half a century. Our object will be to recover their confidence after the conclusion of the hostilities which have ended victoriously for us. So much for the north-western, and the first half of the western frontier, and for Northern Afghanistan.

Let us then consider the southern or lower half of the western frontier, the most vitally important of all parts, and with that view fix our eyes on Sukkur in Sind, far down the Indus in the lower basin of that river. Sukkur was always important in old Moslem times. In these British days it has become a military base of the very first consequence On it would converge, in event of war, the troops and stores from the Panjab and Northern India by the Indus valley railways. To it would be brought, by rail also, the stores, the convoys, the reinforcements of troops from England brought by the fleet of ironclads and transports that might be lying off Kurrachee, near the mouth of the Indus. Now what is the meaning of all this? Well, from Sukkur there branches off almost at a right angle the railway to Quetta in Beluchistan, just beyond the famous Bolan Pass, and thence to the tunnel piercing the mountain range which overlooks Southern Afghanistan, and from the summit of which, by a telescope, can be descried the hills that overlook Candahar. This tunnel is the limit of British dominion in that quarter. From it, in event of need, a military railway could be constructed in a very few weeks to Candahar —the time, indeed, might be counted by days. Why has all this been arranged? Because we must be able to command the routes to and from, in and about, Candahar; and because Candahar is a dominating point on the route by which Russia might advance from Merve through Herat towards India. Indeed, she must advance this way, if she ever advances

POOLS IN THE BOLAN PASS

at all with any chance of success. Therefore we must be in a position to make Candahar an unconquerable base of our warlike operations in defence of the Indian Empire. I will not here dilate on the extraordinary advantages locally which Candahar offers us in this respect. If Russia were to undertake an attack upon, or even a diversion towards India, she might take some route of her own to confound all our calculations. But she would probably take this Candahar route, which does afford certain facilities hardly to be found elsewhere. So we must be prepared accordingly. It is reckoned that she would be beaten on this route; and if so, still more would she be defeated on any other route. In a summary like the present this truly Imperial question cannot be pursued further. Enough has perhaps been said to indicate the character of the lower or southern portion of the western frontier of India.

There yet remains an Indian frontier which has of late been rising in interest, and which might in certain political combinations become of grave importance. Beyond the eastern frontier, already mentioned, lies Burma, now wholly British, and forming an outpost of, or an adjunct to, the Indian Empire. Burma proper is the valley of the Irawady, and its upper or northern part touches on China in the province of Yunan. The mountains in that part are tremendous and imperfectly explored. The contact with the Chinese Empire at this point may possibly prove to be of much consequence commercially, and intercourse between British and Chinese subjects may bring about results of a magnitude difficult to calculate. But this is as yet undeveloped, and the country is reported to be precipitous in the extreme. At all events there is not the remotest fear of any enemy in that direction. In this neighbourhood, however, slightly to the south-east are the upper waters of the Mekhong, the river which, some hundreds of miles to the south, flows into the Gulf of Siam. On the banks of this river there arose some few years ago that quarrel between France and Siam which

RIVER IRAWADY (BURMA)

proved very unfortunate to the latter. Now England has interests in the region whence this mighty river springs, and France claims to make extensions in that quarter also. Consequently there has been, and yet may be, anxiety regarding the relations between the two Powers in this particular quarter. For the present there has been a satisfactory delimitation between the English and French spheres of influence. On the whole, then, Burma—that is, the valley of the Irawady—is safe enough as regards its frontiers, and the base of its power is on the sea near Rangoon.

But to Burma there are joined the provinces of Moulmein, on the Gulf of Martaban, and of Tenasserim, which runs far southwards along the Bay of Bengal towards the Malay Peninsula. To Burma also belong the Shan States. Now these provinces abut on Siam, and consequently England has a strong interest in Siamese independence. She would certainly object to Siam falling under the domination or under the exclusive influence of a European Power like France. In that case there might be something that would be virtually French dominion running for several hundred miles conterminously with the British provinces attached to Burma. If that were allowed, France might ultimately advance further till she touched the upper Mekhong, and so come in contact with some other of the Burmese regions already mentioned besides one or two points which she already touches. The inconvenience of all this for England is too manifest to need explanation, and, under circumstances easily imaginable, it might grow into positive danger. Hence arose the critical discussions which took place in 1895 between England and France regarding the proceedings of the latter towards Siam. Ultimately the arrangement, whereby England and France mutually agreed to respect and to guard the independence of Siam, staved off peril for the present. Still the attitude of France produced a moral effect on Siam, placing the Siamese Sovereign in such a position that nothing could have saved him from French domination except indirect support and protection from England. It is to be hoped that the recent arrangement may keep matters quiet for a while, and preserve to us Siam as a buffer between our long frontier in that quarter, and the French possessions or dependencies at the basin of the Cambodia, of which their colony of Saigon is the capital. But the fact is that the French proceedings in relation to Siam have created a new frontier difficulty for the Indian Empire, and added a fresh load to the already heavy burden of Indian anxieties.

Lastly, as we must significantly note, it is towards Russia that India looks in reference to the western frontier, and towards France in reference to the south-eastern—the two very Powers between whom a combination is thought by many to be possible.

CHAPTER IX

HOW INDIA IS GOVERNED

Machinery of Government—The Viceroy and Governor-General—The Provincial Governors—The District Officers—The Executive and the Judicial authority—The Legislative Councils—The European Officers and the Native establishments—State forests—Railways and public works—The Post Office—The European troops and the Native army—The barracks—The naval force—Administrative achievements—Establishment of order—Social improvement—Enactment of laws—State-aided education—Saving of life in time of famine—Protection of the public health—Progress of agriculture—System of irrigation—Capital outlay on railways.

In the preceding chapter the external politics of India have been sufficiently disposed of, so that we may now deal with the internal government of the Empire, and then summarise the result.

The Government of British India—that is, the territory directly under British administration, apart from the native States already mentioned—comprises a dominion about as large as Europe, exclusive of Russia. Its organisation is, perhaps, the largest in the world. This organisation is divided into three Presidencies: Bengal, Madras, and Bombay, the old divisions which have existed ever since the beginning of British rule. It is perfectly centralised for general and Imperial purposes, and equally well decentralised for local purposes. It is controlled absolutely by the Secretary of State for India in Council in England. But it is conducted in India by the Viceroy and Governor-General in Council. He acts by and with the advice of his Council, but he can in any matter of moment act on his own authority alone; so his power is in effect plenary. There are just a few territories under his immediate administration; otherwise his orders go, not to subordinate officers at all, but to the various provincial governments: those of Madras and Bombay, as Presidencies, whose heads are Governors; those of Bengal, the North-Western Provinces and the Punjab, whose heads are Lieutenant-Governors; those of the Central Provinces, Assam and Burma, whose heads are Chief Commissioners. From these several and various governments the orders go to the many districts, resembling counties in the British Isles. These districts are in most provinces grouped into divisions called commissionerships. Practically before the eyes of the people British rule is represented by the district officers, who are magistrates and tax-gatherers, and by the commissioners. These officers are generally Europeans belonging to the Imperial Civil Service; but sometimes they are military officers, sometimes also officers belonging to branches of the Civil Service other than the Imperial. Occasionally, but rarely, they are natives. By this widespread machinery is the vast administration conducted, and it is called the Executive authority.

But the judicial authority acts in court independently of the Government. Thus the poorest man has his remedy against the richest, and even against the Government itself, in a court of justice. But the courts themselves are constituted, and the judges are appointed, by the Executive. Nevertheless the Executive, even though it be supreme, bows to the decision of its own courts, there being no longer any personal or patriarchal rule. It does not undertake to do anything save under the laws, which laws are interpreted by the courts; but it is influential, almost potential, in making the laws. There is no such thing as absolute authority vested in an individual; everything is done by law alone, though in the due carrying out of the same there is infinite scope for personal ability. In that sense there is immense responsibility on the individual officer for the weal or woe of the people.

There is a chain of judicial authorities, from the lesser judge, who is like a county court judge, to the district judge, and on to the High Court or the Chief Court. The judiciary is separate for each province. The principal judges are mostly Europeans.

The question immediately arises, how are the laws made and who are the law-makers? Everything depends on that. In this matter the Executive has the dominant voice. There is a Supreme Legislative Council of which the Viceroy is President, and which makes laws affecting the whole of India. There are also provincial legislative councils in Madras, Bombay, and Bengal, and there will be councils for other parts as well. These make laws for their respective Provinces. Into all these councils an elective element has, of late years, been cautiously introduced, mainly for the election of native members. But the majority are the nominees of the Executive Government. There is no such thing as voting to order, and the independent opinion of its trusted officers, nominated by itself to sit on these councils, must be respected by the Government. Thus, on the one hand, it would not be possible for the Viceroy and his Executive Council to pass a law opposed strongly by Indian opinion as reflected in the Legislative Council; on the other hand, he would always be sure of a majority in any matter where the Imperial interests of India might be concerned. And as both he and the Secretary of State have a real power of veto, no law could take effect if disapproved by them.

The financial administration is concentrated under the Finance Minister, who is a member of the Viceroy's Executive Council, and who has his representative, called Accountant-General, at the headquarters of every provincial government. There is, however, a provincial finance which is administered independently for each province of the Empire by the provincial government.

The constitution of the Indian Government is fixed entirely by statutes of the English Parliament. Thus, taking it all in all, this system of government is as stable and solid as it could possibly be made.

The principal offices in all branches are filled by Europeans of the best stamp, indeed it has been always held that the Imperial Civil Service of India is, from its status and qualifications, the most important body of the kind in the service of any Government in any country. It is absolutely necessary for the safety of the Empire to maintain European forcefulness and trustworthiness in these positions of national trust. Otherwise, the vast majority of the numberless civil offices in India are filled by natives, and from time to time the promotion of natives to higher and higher offices is increasing. In other words, the mass of the civil servants in India is native; and it is right that natives should have as many appointments as possible in their own country, the headships only being reserved for Europeans, for Imperial reasons of extreme cogency.

Such is the mechanism which extends from the Viceroy to the humblest village official; from the Chief Justice of a High Court down to the smallest local judge; from the capital city to the remotest, even to the wildest corner of the land—which includes the collection of the revenue and of the taxes, the magistracy, police and prisons, the public instruction and national education, and all that which in England is comprised under the head of local government and administration. There are separate establishments for the State forests, already mentioned in a previous Chapter, and for the public works and railways, on a gigantic scale which have yet to be noticed. There is the Post Office, ramifying from the great centres even to the villages throughout the continent; also the electric telegraph, which, though not carried out in so much detail, is yet very extensive. Further, there is a great medical establishment, partly maintained for works of benevolence among the people, with Europeans indeed at the head, but with the ranks filled by natives educated in Western science.

This government is supported by an army of more than 200,000 men, now consisting of five army corps under one Commander-in-Chief. Of these, a proportion of between one-third and one-half consists of Europeans, the remainder being natives. The European troops are of acknowledged excellence, the best, indeed, that the British Isles can produce

—the battalions being made up to full strength with suitable men; the questions about weak battalions which vex the public mind in England being unknown in India. The native troops consist of men who enter the service voluntarily, intending to remain in it during the active years of life. Many of these troops fight side by side with the Europeans in a manner that leaves nothing to be desired. Inside India the European troops are so disposed as to insure to them the mastery of every strategic position, in order that the recurrence of the events of the mutiny of 1857 may be impossible. The artillery is almost entirely in the hands of Europeans. There are in the various parts of India effective corps of volunteers, consisting of Europeans and East Indians. The barracks for European troops are, as military structures, not to be surpassed in any country; they have been called palatial, but their dimensions are of that character which is necessary for the health of the men. The commissariat and transport have long been famous for efficiency on actual service, and in the field.

For the support of the Indian Empire there is a large squadron of the British navy, with its headquarters at Trincomalee, in Ceylon, keeping the peace of the sea in the Persian Gulf, the sea of Arabia, and a part of the Indian Ocean.

As regards these enormous establishments—guided and directed, as I firmly believe, with integrity, honour, public spirit, patriotism, and a single-minded devotion to the welfare of the people—the question arises, what have they done, what are they doing? In other words, what has British rule effected, what is it still effecting?

In the first place, it has secured to the agricultural people—who are the great majority of the nation—immunity from fire and sword, from plunder and devastation, from rack and ruin, from dispersion of families and breaking up of homes. Those who know how rampant these evils were right up to the early part of this century will appreciate the blessing thus conferred. The last generation but one doubtless remembered this vividly, and was proportionately grateful. The last generation was beginning to forget this, but was reminded of it by the recrudescence of horrors more or less in many places during the war of the Mutinies in 1857. The present generation is forgetting, perhaps has already forgotten this, and accordingly the gratitude has faded. But the record of history remains.

It has thus answered for order, and established that which bears the proud title of "Pax Britannica."

It has by persistent exertions stamped out organised crime. The Thug no longer steals along in the dark, like a stealthy tiger, to strangle his victim. The band of dacoit ruffians no longer bursts on a fertile village at midnight to plunder and rob, to beat down resistance with steel and firearms.

It has preserved neutrality and impartiality between the several religions of the country, respecting the endowments made by preceding native rulers to their religious institutions, but withdrawing from any share in the management of the same. Without attempting to act as umpire or arbiter between opposite religions or rival sects, it has prohibited any overt violence being shown by one to the other, any public insult, offence or annoyance. It has repeatedly enforced this prohibition with all its might and promptitude, in the fanatical and deadly feuds which seem destined to rise from time to time, and which, under a weaker government, would attain a grave importance. It has afforded legal facilities regarding marriage and the like to those who have ceased to belong to any of the recognised religions of the country.

It has put an end to the barbarous rites,—like "Sati," or widow burning, female infanticide, human sacrifices among wild tribes. Otherwise it has scrupulously respected all the customs of the people so far as might be consistent with Christian civilisation. The consideration thus shown by it, which was not always shown under native rule, is one among many reasons of the popularity or acquiescence with which it is regarded by the natives.

It has, while professing and avowing its Christianity, refrained from supporting the same among the natives by any resources of, or exercise of power by, the State. It has extended to Christian Missions the same freedom as that enjoyed by other religious bodies, that much and no more. With such freedom the Christian Missions have by their own persuasiveness advanced apace.

It has maintained the pre-existing laws of the several nationalities and communities, but it has legislated on doubtful points, and it has passed just laws for countless matters of wide importance, not covered by the different native systems,—in codes second to none anywhere. By its judiciary and its executive it has provided for the equal administration of these laws between the humblest and the highest. And although it cannot save the poor from their inevitable disadvantages in conflict with the rich, yet the amazing litigiousness of the natives, even down to the humblest classes, shows how much they appreciate the impartiality of a judicial system unknown in any like degree under native rulers.

It has made all classes, especially the middle and lower, confident in the possession of whatever they can save or accumulate, in bullion or in kind. It has thus caused the hoarded wealth and the capital of the nation to grow enormously, and has enabled the native bankers, always potent in the cities, to spread, perhaps overmuch, throughout the villages.

It has recognised and rendered effectually valuable, though it did not create, the property in land, in a long series of degrees, whether the tenant right, or the peasant proprietorship, or the landlord status, or the privilege of the superior rent collector. It has by a public registration of tenures, corrected yearly for every village, rendered every one sure of his title, whether to a small holding, or an estate, or a territorial domain. To this end it has effected a survey of every field. It has thus caused this property, which had a fitful and struggling existence during the past ages, like an old flag, riddled, torn, battered, to wave a standard throughout the land.

It has rendered this property worth having by an equitable limitation of the State demand for land tax, in perpetuity for some provinces and for long terms of years in others, leaving a margin for subsistence and for profit to the owner larger than any margin ever left before under native rulers.

It has improved among the native public servants that integrity, the want of which was ever the crying fault of native administration, by increased emoluments, by prospects of promotion, by assurance of pension, by civil discipline, by general elevation of status.

It has set up, for all creeds and races alike, a system of State-aided education with universities, colleges, secondary schools, and village schools, which system, though far from complete, is constantly extending, has deeply touched the upper classes, largely affected the middle classes, and spread considerably though not fully among the humbler classes. It has instituted a public instruction which communicates sound knowledge not only in English but in the many Indian languages, thus creating amultiform, indeed a gigantic vernacular literature, an achievement which transcends anything previously known under native rulers.

It has carried out principles of sanitation in all cities and towns, often with drainage works and waterworks on a magnificent scale ; all which, despite the occasional outbreaks of disease that defy foresight and calculation, has benefited the public health and almost extirpated diseases previously endemic. In combination with this, it has, by establishing medical dispensaries charitably and gratuitously throughout the interior of the country, exemplified the care which the State feels for its people, and imbued them with some practical notion of Christian charity.

It has acknowledged the duty and obligation of the State to save the people from the consequences of the drought and famine which periodically appear. It has spent vast sums of money and applied all its administrative power to this humane purpose, with success sometimes complete, at other times partial, but at all times with the conviction produced on the national mind that the utmost possible had been done.

It has introduced the idea of local self-government by giving the municipal franchise to Calcutta, Bombay and other cities, after the European model. In some provinces it has set up what would in England be called district councils. It has cautiously and sparingly appointed deserving men to be honorary magistrates.

It has liberated trade from transit dues, and the taxpayer from oppressive imposts tyrannically levied, concentrating its own taxation on a few main heads after the English model.

It has with an outlay of capital, vast even from an English point of view, set up a system of irrigation, the grandest in engineering conception, the noblest in scientific skill that has been seen in any age or country. The Indian rivers — the five rivers of the Panjab, the Ganges and the Jamna, the

Godavery, the Kistna, and the Cauvery, and others — have been rendered the tributaries and the servants of agriculture.

Its road making was in full swing at the time when railways were introduced, and some of its trunk lines of road were of vast length and often remarkable in alignment. This work has been partly superseded by the railways, but the network of district roads continues to spread.

It has, with capital raised in England, caused railways to be constructed, so as to connect and bind together all the principal places throughout the continent, with many engineering works of the first magnitude, viaducts over big rivers and broad flood-basins, and inclines with stiff gradients up mountain-sides.

It has carried out scientific work of magnitude yet of intricacy and minuteness in the trigonometrical survey, the geological survey, the Botanical Gardens, the meteorological observations.

Such, in the most brief and rapid summary,

is what British rule has heretofore essayed to do and actually done. It is daily attempting and accomplishing more and more, never satisfied with progress made up to date, but ever striving to advance further. In the next chapter I shall consider how far the results in regard to the national condition have been commensurate with all this action.

CHAPTER X

PROGRESS OF INDIA UNDER BRITISH RULE

Remarkable increase of population—Yet the density per square mile not great—Expansion and improvement of cultivation—Irrigation by canals—Property in land—Public health and sanitation—Mitigation or prevention of famine—Old industries disappearing and new ones springing up—Jute and cotton, tea and coffee—Coal mines—Ocean-borne trade, coasting traffic, river navigation—State revenues and receipts—Public debt—Disposition of the people towards British rule—Progress of Christianity among the natives—National education — Disturbing elements politically—Some fanaticism and bigotry—Causes of discontent—Countervailing causes of loyalty—Net result favourable—Permanent and inevitable dangers—Need of watchfulness.

THE organisation of British rule in India, and the administrative achievements of the Government during the nineteenth century, have been briefly described in the preceding chapter. It remains, in continuation, to summarise the results of this administration and its effects on the progress of the country at large, including the British territories and the native States.

In the first place there has been an enormous increase of population in India as a whole. The only element of doubt is this: that complete enumerations have been had only since the middle of this century. Before that the population used to be calculated district by district. Therefore, though fairly certain as to the population during the last two generations, we are not so sure as to what it was during previous generations. For a summary like the present it is better to take the entire dominion, British territories and native States together, because then all questions regarding conquest and annexation disappear, and there is no need to reckon the transfer of whole peoples from native States to British territories, and so forth. Reckoned in its truly grand total, the population amounted, according to the last decennial census of 1890, to two hundred and eighty-seven millions of souls, showing the wondrous increase over the previous decade of thirty-five millions, of which a small portion only was attributable to the annexation of Upper Burma, while the rest must have arisen from natural increment. In the decade before that the increase was shown at less than fifteen millions, but then that was a period of famine. In general terms it may be said that in this century, during the Queen's reign, the population has increased by one hundred millions. By reference to calculations made during the earlier part of the century in one province and another from time to time, the increase may be assumed to have been over 50,000,000. Thus the increase of 150,000,000 in the continent and peninsula during one century is a matter for wonderment as well as congratulation. There is room, too, in the country for all these mighty numbers, for as yet the population is less than 200 to the square mile.

This teeming population has been, and is, sustained by an expansion and an improvement of cultivation. This expansion has been great in the hilly country of the central and eastern parts of the continent. It has been most marked in the eastern parts of Bengal, which may be called the lower basin of the Brahmaputra. The improvement arises from the introduction of irrigation by various canal systems already mentioned. Not only is the produce thus secured against drought, but also superior crops are cultivated. In these ways the agricultural sustenance of the population has vastly increased.

The property in land having been secured by elaborate arrangements, as explained in a previous Chapter, the selling, the mortgaging, the transferring of real property goes on rapidly. Land has now a saleable value unknown before. The wages of agricultural labour have risen from 30 to 40 per cent.

Further, the growth of numbers has been promoted by an improvement in the public health. Although epidemic outbreaks unaccountably occur, still many fell diseases, which used to be endemic or abiding, have become sporadic or casual. Other diseases which used to be destructive, have been mitigated in violence or virulence, though they can never be prevented altogether. All this is owing to the municipal works for water supply and for drainage previously mentioned, to sanitary precautions when great assemblages are collected on pilgrimage and the like, to the establishment of medical dispensaries in the interior of the country, and to the development of a native medical profession on European models.

The prevention, or the restriction, or the mitigation of famine, though it may not have succeeded in preventing a considerable loss of life, has yet greatly checked the loss which might otherwise have occurred, has saved innumerable persons from death, families from dispersion, homes from ruin, property from wastage. Thus the population has not been decimated in the same manner which might otherwise have been apprehended.

The industry of the people, though greatly modified in many directions, has yet thriven and prospered immensely. Some elegant and exquisite industries for which India was once renowned have disappeared, or have shrunk before the advance of English-made piece goods. Some beautiful arts have been lost altogether. Still, many such industries, in wood inlaid, in horns, in metals, in enamel, in pottery, in silk, and in many other things survive for the admiration of Western nations. On the other hand, new industries, chiefly textile, in cotton, jute, and the like, have sprung up with Indian material and labour, but with European capital, machinery, and supervision.

In the same way new products, such as tea and coffee, are raised in the mountain tracts bordering both the continent and the peninsula. Mining in coal and iron has in some localities been successfully developed. The wages of artisans have risen even more than those of the agricultural labourers.

The trade, both as regards inland traffic and ocean-borne commerce, has multiplied, largely in consequence of the railways, which have quite changed the character of the inland traffic, and have rendered infinite assistance to the commerce destined for ocean transit. The ocean-borne commerce, now carried mainly by steamers through the Suez Canal, and partly by sailing ships and steamers round the Cape of Good Hope, has risen within the Queen's reign from £20,000,000 sterling in annual value to £200,000,000. It brings vast quantities of British manufactures into India, thus constituting India the best customer that Britain has in the world. It carries still greater quantities of Indian produce, including wheat, to England for consumption there. The coasting traffic round the coasts of the peninsula was always great, but has been much developed by steamers during the last half century. The boat traffic on some rivers, like the Indus and the Ganges, has given way before the railways. In other rivers, like those which permeate Eastern Bengal, it has thriven amazingly, in a manner perhaps equalled in China, but nowhere else.

The revenues and receipts of the Government have increased fourfold since the time when the countries now forming the British territories were conquered, ceded or annexed. They now amount to a total which would be reckoned at nearly one hundred millions sterling annually according to the old way of reckoning, but which is now reckoned in rupees x, or tens of rupees. Though no exact comparison can be made, yet historical calculations indicate that a sum total not much inferior to this may have been raised over the same area under native rule, when the population, the trade, the agriculture and the taxable resources were all much less than they are now. Calculations of this nature cannot be depended on; still they do confirm the opinion, which is supported on other ground, to the effect that the natives of India are lightly taxed, much more leniently indeed than under any rulers preceding the British. The public debt amounts to three hundred millions sterling, equal to little more than the revenues and receipts of the Government for three years, of this nine-tenths have been subscribed by the London money market, and one-tenth by the natives of India. The greater part has been incurred for remunerative works of national utility, and the lesser part for war. Besides this sum, European capital, to an amount variously estimated, but reckoned at two hundred and fifty millions sterling, has been invested in a hundred enterprises throughout India.

After this summary of progress, material and mental, there follows the profound question regarding the temper and disposition of the various classes of the vast population towards the British Government, and the loyalty of the people at large.

These material results have affected the whole mind of the people. The cessation of trouble from without has caused their thoughts to be turned towards domestic comfort and towards industry of every sort. The excitability which used to be roused by war and revolution now finds its vent in excessive litigation. We cannot define the effect produced by the State-aided education on the millions of children that have been gathered into the schools of town and country. It must have rendered the rising generation more reasonably thoughtful and more practically skilful. But, in the absence of legal compulsion on the parents to send their children to school, there are many more millions of possible scholars yet to be gathered in. Moreover, the instruction tends too much towards literature and too little towards physical science. The status of woman, under educational influences, has been raised and improved. The influence of Western knowledge on the religion of the Hindus has been mentioned in a previous Chapter.

Christianity has been firmly rooted among the natives in some districts of the southern peninsula and of the hill tracts near Bengal. It has also been planted in many centres like Benares, Agra, Delhi, and in a score of localities of the interior. This work has been done by the Christian Missions, Protestant, despatched from Britain in the nineteenth century. The Roman Catholic Missions, mainly of Portuguese origin, were established in Western India and elsewhere during the seventeenth and eighteenth centuries; and their work still survives.

However strong may be the grounds for confidence on the whole, we must never shut our eyes to the fact that there are, and perhaps ever will be, disturbing elements. However sure we may be that the great majority are loyal, yet there is, and long will be, a considerable minority who are disloyal.

No doubt there are fanatical Moslem preachers who will make no terms with the Cross before which the Crescent is fast waning. Some learned and severely orthodox Hindus will have no *modus vivendi* with those Western influences that are destroying Brahminism. There are classes everywhere, limited in numbers but strong in spirit, who once carved out their fortunes by armed force, and are now condemned to continue in scarceness and in quietude. Worse still, there are many ambitious men, who might have had careers and won positions in a revolutionary era, who are now eating their hearts out under a system of examination and competition and of fitness acquired by education. Even more important are the descendants of the hereditary office-bearers and Ministers, of the retainers and dependents of native States and dynasties that have been conquered, or annexed, or dispossessed, during many wars and campaigns. There are many families scattered all over the country, with large and influential connections, with traditions of wealth and power, and yet with but little hope under a foreign domination. Certain races or tribes, here and there, are doubtless under the impression that they might strike a blow for their own domination, if, by any circumstances either in India itself, or in Europe, or in any part of the world, the British Government were to be shaken. Notably among these are many Mahratta leaders in Western India who look wistfully to the days when their national hero, Sivaji, rebelled successfully against the Moslem power and re-established a Hindu Empire for India. Moreover, there are persons in every part of the country, who are certainly numerous, but whose number cannot be reckoned, and who love their own indigenous rule, however faulty, and hate foreign rule, even though it be comparatively perfect. These would fling away the blessings they enjoy under us, for the sake of once more seeing the old Sovereign enthroned, the old priesthood in high places, the old titles resounding in the air, and this, too, despite all perils which such attempted changes might bring about. Behind all these classes and sections is the mob in all the principal cities, stations, and even cantonments, ever ready to join in a general fight if the bonds of order should be loosened. The aggregate of all these disturbing elements is considerable. Much, perhaps most of it, too, cannot be mitigated or averted by any measures, however beneficent, by any steps that an alien Government could take. These difficulties are inherent in the nature of the case, from our Imperial point of view, and we must be ever ready to meet them, never allowing them to escape our recollection.

But as against these inevitable disadvantages, the known advantages should be summed up. In the first place, as explained in a previous chapter, the native States, that is, the native Princes and chiefs, are actively loyal to the Indian Empire. It does not follow that they could always control all the classes in their territories. But the fact that the ruling and guiding classes—princes, chiefs, retainers, dependents, establishments—who govern some sixty millions of their own people, and are highly regarded by scores and scores of millions in British territories, should be positively on our side, is a great political gain.

The landlords in many provinces, in whose estates the land revenue tax has been lightly fixed, either in perpetuity or for long terms of years, have strong interests bound up with the British Government.

The capitalists and bankers, the money markets and commercial chambers, the moneyed classes, who while having their centres in the towns and cities do yet branch out to the remotest parts of the country, are all strongly for the British Government, and would bring immense resources to its aid.

The peasant proprietors, the largest class of all the classes in the country, are at least passively loyal. They have their property secured to them in a manner never known before; they must naturally wish to keep what they have got. But with their ancestral tradition of submitting to the rule of the day, be it bad or good, they are not demonstrative even in their loyalty.

Much the same may be said of the labourers on the farms and fields, of the artisans, of the hands in factories; they are thankful for their improved condition; their acquiescence in the foreign rule is valuable, but they do not represent any active force on our side.

Thus the sum total of the loyal greatly exceeds in weight that of the disloyal. But the quality of Indian loyalty, though among many individuals and with some classes it cannot be surpassed anywhere, is not the same as that of British loyalty to the British Government, that which arises from flesh and blood, from community of race, creed and colour. It might not stand the ordeal of disaster ; it might fade before the prestige of an enemy victorious over England. Still, so long as we hold our own, it is a tower of strength to us.

There is an increasing unrest among the classes who have been educated under the Western system, though the general loyalty of these classes may be affirmed. They form organisations, under the names of congresses and suchlike associations, in order to formulate requests to the Government, of which some may be worthy of favourable consideration, while others will be found incompatible with the preservation of British supremacy.

Thus, while the Indian Empire is safe according to all calculations that could ordinarily be made, though there is much more of strength than of weakness in this structure, still there are abiding dangers both from within and without. Such dangers are of periodical occurrence, will frequently recur, are not likely ever to cease within any time to which we can reasonably look forward. Doubtless the stability of our rule largely depends on good governance, on the loyalty of some classes, on the contentment and acquiescence of the great majority. Behind all this, however, there must be the universal knowledge that armed force exists in adequate strength. India is essentially a land of risks and of perils. The risks will, we trust, be avoided, and the perils surmounted in the future, as they have been on numberless occasions during the past. No exaggerated apprehension should be entertained when troubles shall arise which, after all, are similar to those which have occurred before, and have been invariably overcome. According to the dictum of a most illustrious man, they will come on in the old way, and will be beaten off in the old way. But the watchfulness, which has rarely failed us as yet, must never be relaxed. Any tampering with Imperial safety, even from the most benevolent motives, is to be strenuously deprecated. Not only must the strength of the European troops be adequately sustained under the best commanders that can be found, but also the establishment of European civil and political officers must be maintained in the highest possible efficiency.

CHAPTER XI

HISTORIC REMAINS AND RUINS

Obscurity of antique history in India—Prehistoric remains—Ancient immigration of the Hindus—The Vedas, the epic "Mahabbharat," and the "Ramayana" of the hero Rama—The Code of Manu—The Brahmanic religion established—Overthrown by the Boodhist Reformation—Personality of Booddha—His religion established—Greek invasion by Alexander the Great—Inroads by Greek, Bactrian, and Scythian rulers—Their ultimate expulsion under Chandra Gupta and Vikramaditya—Booddhist Empire under King Asoka—Overthrow of Booddhism and re-establishment of Brahmanism—Moslem invasion in the eleventh century—Rise and progress of the Mogul Empire—Uprising of the Hindu Mahrattas—The Mahratta Empire—Succeeded by the British Empire—Ruins and remains—Of the Booddhist era—Of the restored Brahmanic era—Of the Moslem times—The present—British architecture.

We have now briefly reviewed the country, the people, the government, mentioning all, or nearly all, that is absolutely necessary to be known by a visitor who would travel rapidly in India with intellectual advantage, or by a general reader—though the outline which I have drawn admits of being filled in with infinite details should there be sufficient time for such study. Still, such a person would, in the course of his travel or his reading, either see, or hear of, or read about ruins and ancient remains so numerous, so fine and grand, so varied, so indicative of distinct races, civilisations, and social systems, as naturally to excite a curiosity to learn the historic arrangement of these phenomena, and to discern at least the framework of the complex story. The subject is indeed so immense that it cannot be treated in a book of this nature with even the most distant approach to completeness. Nevertheless, something like an intelligible abstract may be presented within our short space.

Few persons could imagine, except those who have had to investigate, how misty and obscure the ancient history of India is, from the antique beginning down to the eleventh century after the Christian era. From that century onwards it is so elaborate as to perplex the student with details. Before that century he can pick up nothing save noble fragments which he finds it difficult or impossible to piece together.

It is well known that, before the Hindu immigration into India many centuries before the Christian era, there was an indigenous population, probably scanty and scattered, whom the ethnologists designate as Dravidian. Some millions of them are still to be found under the name of aborigines. Some millions more have long ago been incorporated with the humblest caste of the Hindus, after the Hindu immigration in the Vedic era. Anterior to them, however, there must have been a people sometimes called Scythian, but not as yet classed under any nomenclature accepted by ethnology. Their existence is demonstrated by rude monuments and apparently sepulchral structures, which the antiquaries nowadays call "menhirs" and "dolmens," also by primitive implements of various materials. Traces of this sort are seen among the Assam hills in the north-east corner of India, amidst the mountain ranges which form the backbone of the Indian continent, and doubtless more things of the same kind have been, and will be, discovered in other parts of the country. The style of these is either identical with, or similar to, that of monuments and remains of this very kind in other climes, other latitudes, and other quarters of the world. The consideration of this would open out a vista of speculation and inquiry quite beyond the scope of this book.

The original immigration from Central Asia, or the ancient Ariana, into India of that wonderful race subsequently known as the Hindus has been already mentioned in Chapter V. They were then probably but a comparatively scanty band, or several bands, one following the other. They have, in the course of perhaps three thousand years, become the most numerous nationality now on earth ; and, fortunately for them, they are all under the British Sovereign. Their national constitution in the remote beginning, to which they nowadays look back as the golden age, is set forth in the Sanskrit Vedas, which are regarded as among the most valuable records of early mankind, of the *juventus mundi*. There are epics, such as the "Mahabharat," which seem to present at least as good an idea of the ancient Hindus as the Homeric poems do of the earliest Greeks. There is the "Ramayana," describing the actions of Rama, who is deified as the national hero, like Hercules of the Greeks, and who was probably the first Hindu explorer and conqueror in Indian regions, now mostly cultivated, but then primæval jungles sparsely inhabited by aboriginal races. The first capital of Hindu dominion on any extended scale was at Ayodhya in Oudh, not far from the base of the Himalaya. Later on the Code of Manu was compiled and promulgated; and it is among the best examples of antique legislation, civil and religious. The Brahmins, being the priestly tribe or caste among the Hindus, as already explained in Chapter V., established a Brahmanic religion. It flourished for some centuries, and became corrupt. Then it was reformed by Booddha, who set up in its stead the well-known religion named Booddhism.

The facts relating to Booddha are somewhat in this wise. A young prince of ardent imagination and highly strung sensibility was struck by the sight of human suffering and sorrow. He quitted his father's palace somewhere in North Behar, near Oudh, turned his back on the glittering capital of Ayodhya, and went forth in the humblest guise to do good among all sorts and conditions of men. He gathered around him disciples of like temperament, assumed the title of Booddha (a Sanskrit word meaning abstract wisdom), preached pure morality, and continued in this course to his end. His reformed religion grew fast, overturned Brahmanism, and became the State religion in most parts of India.

Then Alexander and his Macedonians

burst into India, in the third century before the Christian era, and defeated King Porus on the bank of the Jhelum in the Panjab. He must have found a Booddhistic rather than a Brahmanic India. Then followed a series of foreign rulers from beyond Afghanistan, probably from Bactria—around the Balkh of later ages—who ruled over Western and North-western India. Some of them were called Saka or Scythian, and some were Greek. In the absence of record, several, if not most, of these separate dynasties can be traced by their coins, which have been found in great abundance. This elucidation of a history, otherwise almost unknown, is among the triumphs of numismatic science. It is probable that these foreigners of Central Asian race adopted the Booddhism of the India where they were settled. Nevertheless, they were all ultimately driven out of India by the Indians. In this national effort two names were conspicuous and are to this day remembered, one being Chandra Gupta, whom the Greeks called Sandracotus; the other being Vikramaditya; but it is to be remembered that Vikramaditya is a dynastic title, and there were other great Vikramadityas besides this one.

Thus Booddhism prospered mightily in India. In itself originally a reformation, it became in its turn corrupted. A Booddhist dominion which might almost be called an empire was established in Northern India under King Asoka. The story can be dimly traced by coins, rock inscriptions, scanty records and notices by foreign or collateral authorities.

The corrupted Booddhism was, some considerable time after the Christian era, overthrown, and Brahmanism was restored. Of this change, again, the record is meagre, though much evidence is derivable from noble ruins and remains. The new Brahmanic capital was set up probably at Ujjain, not far from Gwalior in the direction of the Jamna. During that era was composed most of that beautiful Sanskrit poetry which has since delighted the world of learning. The Brahmanic system then flourished in much splendour throughout India till the eleventh century. There was, however, an offshoot of Booddhism, named the Jain religion, which retained its purity and survived the overthrow of Booddhism. It exists in wealth and influence to this day. Its sacred architecture is famed for beauty of style.

In the year 1001 A.D. the Moslem Mahmud of Ghuznee burst into India and established the faith of Islam at Delhi by force of arms. This action of his changed the face of India during several centuries. The history of India, thenceforward elaborately recorded, becomes complex owing to the multiplicity and rapid succession of Moslem dynasties greater and less. But it was terribly simplified when in the sixteenth century Akber, commonly called the Great—and his title Akber is an Arabic word, meaning the Great—subdued most of these dynasties and established in India that which is known in Europe as the Empire of the Great Mogul. He was doubtless the greatest native ruler ever seen in India. Previously there is not known any one equal to him; nor afterwards was there any ruler like him till the Englishman, Warren Hastings, appeared on the scene. All this time the Hindu religion was recognised, but if there was such a thing as a State religion it was that of Islam. After Akber the Mogul Empire flourished resplendently for a century and more, and then began to decay. During this decadence some of the old Moslem States again reared their heads and new Moslem States arose under the lieutenants of the Great Mogul.

Next, midway in the seventeenth century, the Hindu Sivaji, a Mahratta, raised the standard of Hinduism in rebellion against Islam, both as regards its faith and its domination. Thus was established a Mahratta Empire on the ruins of that which belonged to the Great Mogul. A Mahratta confederacy was formed by Hindus of the lower caste under a hereditary head, a Brahmin styled the Peshwa. So there actually was for several generations a Brahmin or priestly dynasty, a circumstance unique in Indian history. Afterwards there were Afghan and Persian invasions under able leaders. At length the Mahrattas assembled for decisive action in the middle of the eighteenth century. They were defeated at Panipat, not far from Delhi. Their empire thus received a deadly blow, but still survived for a while till it was beaten piecemeal by the advancing power of the British.

From the flood of confusion on the downfall of the Mogul Empire, the Sikh faith reared its head in the Panjab. It was really a local reformation of Hinduism, and ultimately dominated that important province.

The British dominion founded under Clive and Hastings, developed under Wellesley, gradually embraced or overshadowed the whole country, both the continent and the peninsula, till the year 1877, when it was formally proclaimed to be an Empire, under Queen Victoria as Empress.

In this summary sketch of an enormous

story, seven Indian names stand forth to be remembered first of all by the student, namely —Rama for early Hinduism—Booddha for the great Reformation—Asoka for Imperial Booddhism—Chandra Gupta (called Sandacotus by the Greeks) who expelled the foreigners—Vikramaditya, the principal ruler under the restored Brahmanism—Akber for Islam with toleration of the revived Hinduism—Sivaji, the originator of the revolt against Moslem domination in India. So also there are six epochs of Indian splendour, each being more splendid than the one before it—I. the establishment of Ayodhya, how many centuries before Christ none can say for certain ; II. the year before the death of Asoka, about three hundred years before the Christian era ; III. the time immediately before the year 1001 A.D., just before the first Muhammadan invasion ; IV. the close of the reign of Akber the Great in 1605 ; V. the culmination of the Mahratta power before the fatal battle of Panipat in 1701 ; VI. the proclamation of Queen Victoria as Empress of all India in 1877.

HINDU TEMPLE, BINDRABAN

Let us now consider how far ruins and ancient remains, more or less historical, will help to elucidate the history. These are apart from the prehistoric monuments which are small and scattered, and belong to races as yet wholly unknown even after all the antiquarian research that has been carried on.

Upon the immense history, as sketched above in the lightest manner, the ruins and ancient remains throw a light which cannot be obtained by any other means. They make things known, at least partially, which would have been otherwise unknown. They introduce some clearness into matters which would have been otherwise quite obscure. They render possible some distinctions among affairs which would otherwise have been almost undistinguishable one from the other. They are, indeed, the handmaids of Indian history.

Whether there are any ruins of the Brahmanic time before the Booddhist Reformation we hardly know. There must have been many such, but authentic traces of them are not found. The succeeding Booddhist time, however, is rich in these memorials. The noble tower of Booddh Gya, not far from Patna in Behar, still rears itself aloft as an ornament of that era. The Bhilsa Tope, near Bhopal in Central India, is a mighty mound once encased in stone, surmounted by some towering structure, and surrounded at the base with a circular corridor in massive stonework, with four lofty gateways, one facing each quarter of the compass, each gateway being decorated with fantastic carvings of men and elephants. The rock-cut temple or cave near the summit of the Western Ghaut mountains at Karli, with pillars surmounted by elephants in stone, is the most artistic thing of its kind yet known to us anywhere, and presents a sight of almost unique interest. The series of caves or rock-hewn temples at Ajanta is a wondrous work. In some of these the interior is adorned by frescoes much defaced from neglect rather than from lapse of time. But enough remain in full preservation of form

BOODDHIST TOWER AT BOODH GYA

HINDU TEMPLE NEAR ISLAMABAD IN CASHMERE

and colour to afford priceless evidence of the costumes and the eeremonies of that era. Booddhist architecture was more artistic than anything which has superseded or succeeded it, being signalised by purity and simplicity of taste, by boldness of design, by mastery of outline, even as regards the human form.

The restoration of Brahmanism is attested by the ruins of several temples, and even these remains are magnificent objects. The principal are the ruins of grey stone at Islamabad (or Martand) in Cashmere ; at Biudraban near Agra (or Mathra), of red stone ; of the Black Pagoda on the sea-shore of Orissa, so called by our sailors, who used it as a landmark from the sea; at Bijayanagar, in the midst of a ruined city far to the south at the beginning of the peninsula. The most notable monument of this era consists of the rock-hewn temples or caves at Ellora. They are of the same general design as the caves of Ajanta, but more elaborately ornamented. One rock - cut temple at Ellora is indeed among the chief wonders of India. Vast cuttings were in the first made in the rocky hillside, serving as passages around a mass of rock, which was thus left a *rudis indigestaque moles.* Then this solid mass was operated upon; vast chambers were excavated out of it; then carvings were executed over the whole of the interior and exterior, which thus became a sculptured surface. Then almost indelible colours were painted over the dark stone by an art now lost. Later on, the iconoclastic Moslems tried to burn this colouring away, but in vain. On the outer side of the surrounding passages above mentioned were excavated cells for monks. The sculptured caves on the island of Elephanta, near Bombay, are of the same epoch.

There are naturally many fine Hindu temples, erected many years ago but uninterruptedly used and still flourishing. Some are surmounted by the well-known "Shiwâla," a sort of tower deeply fluted, gently swelling on the sides, slightly tapering towards the top, and completed by a circular coronetted finial. The best types of these are at Jaganath in Orissa, and at Benares, though the best temple there was demolished by order of the Emperor Aurangzebe. The handsomest temple now in use is the one in Nepaul, already mentioned in Chapter VI. In the south—which has been less subjected than the north to foreign invasion—the temples, though old, are still intact, being in full use; they have enclosures with lofty and gigantic gateways covered with sculptures, and called Goparums.

The remains of the early Moslems in India are abundant. Those near old Delhi—at some little distance from the present Delhi—cover several square miles of ground, and though in silent decay, are eloquent regarding departed dynasties. Those in Goojerat, on the western coast, in and about Ahmednagar, are quaint and angular in style, but very fine and instructive. Those in the Deccan, down south, are to be found in several places, and are all beautiful in a high degree. Among them the chief are at Beejapur, which possesses the grandest dome ever erected in the world. The Mogul structures—which are to all other Moslem structures what the poems of Virgil and Horace were to all other Roman poetry — cannot be termed ruins at all. Recognising the exalted position which they hold in the architecture of all nations, the British Government either carries out or supervises the repair of most, though not all, of them. Thus the very best, both at Agra and Delhi, are completely preserved. The structures at Lucknow do not deserve mention, inasmuch as their style, though pretentious, is debased.

This Chapter may be concluded by a few words on the British architecture of the present, which are not historic remains as yet, whatever they may become hereafter. The public structures at Calcutta, Madras, and Bombay are magnificent, and hold their due place in a land so renowned for architecture as India. In other places, and especially in the Native States, buildings are being erected, from designs by European architects, but with a beautiful adaptation of several Eastern styles. This combined or mixed style bears the name of Indo-Saracenic.

CHAPTER XII

EPISODES IN INDIAN HISTORY AND THEIR LOCALITIES

Historic sites—Battlefield of Panipat, near Delhi—Ancient city of Ayodhya—The Indus at Attok—Scene of Alexander's battle with Porus—Situation of ancient Ujjain—The ruins of old Delhi—Desert of Rajputâna and the youthful Akber—Last abode of Akber the Great—Death scene of the Emperor Jehangir—Shah Jehan's last view of the Taj Mehal—Tomb of Aurangzebe—Pertabgurh citadel and Sivajis' revolt—Military position of Arcot, Vellore, and Trichinopoly—Breach in the walls of Seringapatam—Lake at Poona and the last of the Peshwas—Battlefields of Moodki, Ferozshah, and Sobraon, near the Satlej—Battlefields of Chillianwala and Goojerat, between the rivers Jhelum and Chenab—Scenes of the Mutinies at Delhi and the Cashmere Gate—The Residency of Lucknow and its defence

In continuation of the preceding Chapter on the history of India with its visible remains, and in conclusion of the whole subject as treated in this book, it may be well to

GRANITE MONUMENT OF SACRED BULL AT TANJORE

mention some of the chief episodes in this history as they can be understood by any one who visits the spots or places of the occurrences. It is by such visits that the events are more vividly understood than they would otherwise be, that the chain of circumstances is apprehended with comparative ease, and that the whole case comes home to the imagination. With this view we shall take the episodes and their localities, as landmarks of history, not in their geographical but in their historical order. Inasmuch as the topics of this Chapter relate to those of the preceding one, the two Chapters should be conveniently read together, so that there may be no need for repetition.

The first locality thus to be taken is the plain of Panipat just to the west of Delhi. This is certainly the most ancient and the greatest battle-ground in all India. There are no external features to recommend it. A broad, flat, steppe-like plain is all that meets the eye. Still it possesses the character which such plains always have in combination with sky effects, especially in the effulgence of an Eastern sunset. Here was fought the contest narrated in the epic "Mahabharat," which contest really was an inter-tribal struggle between two sections of the early Hindus. Here, too, were fought two battles which had the effect of establishing the Empire of the Great Mogul. Here, again, was the battle of A.D. 1761, whereby the Mahratta Empire was broken by Moslem force. Near here were conducted several of the operations which led to the success of the British efforts to recapture Delhi in 1857, and to surmount the crisis of the mutinies.

Next let us observe Ayodhya in the north of Oudh, a classic name which afterwards appeared in the somewhat corrupt form of Ajudhia. Though nothing can now be seen but gigantic mounds, palatial foundations, and the remnant of street alignment, still the dimensions and design of the city are astonishing if the remoteness of the epoch be considered. Here were the walls, gateways, temples, palaces of a city which was celebrated in the glowing terms of ancient romance, and of which a vision abides in the mind of every devout Hindu to this day. If not here, at least not far from here, was born and bred Booddha, the religious reformer. Here certainly was the scene of many actions in the public life of himself and his disciples.

It may be that no particular spot can now be identified with the reign of Asoka, the Booddhist Emperor. So the next historical locality in our review will be the Khyber Pass and the Indus at Attok. These physical features, which ever dominate both traffic and strategy, are changeless throughout the ages. Down south the channel of the Indus is deflected and modified by every annual inundation; but here in the north it is determined by the everlasting hills. Thus we can view the mountain-portals through which Alexander the Great burst into India. The river-crossing at Attock, the rock-walls, the profoundly deep channel, the volume of water rushing silently though swiftly, are now as they were when the Macedonian boat-bridge must have been constructed. We British had similar boat-bridges there ourselves during many winter seasons since 1850, before the railway viaduct was finished. We can follow Alexander onwards to the river Jhelum and make out the battlefield, near a range of low wooded hills, where he vanquished King Porus—which is nearly the same as the scene of our own battle with the Sikhs at Chillianwala during the second Panjab War. We may accompany him even to the bank of the Satlej, where his Macedonians murmured, saying, "Thus far and no farther," and whence he turned his face back towards Persia.

Whether the site of Ujjain, near the river Jamna, in the direction of Gwalior, can be identified, may be a question; some remains, however, are indicated to this day. If it can, then one of the most historical sites in all India would be there, as marking the period when, after a long series of Central Asian invasions, the dominion of India was recovered by the Hindus.

After that no sites can be connected with the story of the centuries till after the year 1000 A.D. Around Delhi, kingdom after kingdom was set up in perplexing variety, which the general student can hardly follow, except by walking or riding round the ruins of old Delhi near the Delhi of recent centuries, as already mentioned in the preceding Chapter.

But after the accession of the Great Moguls to their throne of empire the historical situations become marked. The desert of Western Rajputana is well known, through which the young Akber was borne in haste by his mother. Little, perhaps, did the members of that little cavalcade dream of the imperial fortunes which they were carrying. In and about Agra may be noticed the very chambers where in his last years the Emperor Akber tried to educe an eclectic faith from the conflicting advocates of various religions. His successor Jehangir loved and adorned the Vale of Cashmere. When dying he yearned to behold the Happy Valley, and was borne thither across the mountains. But he did not reach farther than a place (Behramgul) deep in their very bosom. There amidst gloomy forests, with the azure sky overhead, on a green sward overhanging a rivulet foaming white and glistening with ceaseless motion, may to this day be seen the death-place of a Great Mogul. In the fortress of Agra we may stand in the outer balcony, overlooking the river Jamna with the matchless outline of the Taj Mehal standing forth against the sky. Hither was the third Great Mogul — a prisoner in his own fortress by command of his own son and heir—borne in order to behold in his last moments that unrivalled structure, the glory of his reign and the tomb of his domestic happiness. In the distant south—not far from the Caves of Ellora, already mentioned, may be seen the humble tomb of Aurangzebe, the fourth and last of the Great Moguls, without canopy, and exposed to the weather according to Moslem orthodoxy. As the Emperor was carried hither, broken in health, in spirits, and in

PERTABGURH ROCK FORTRESS

power, having failed to quell the Mahratta rebellion and to subdue the refractory Moslem princes in the south, he pathetically said that he had made his final march. This place is indeed the grave of all that was great in an empire and a dynasty.

The beginning of the Hindu Mahratta insurrection against the Moslems, and of the Mahratta domination afterwards, may be distinctly perceived at Pertabgurh near Mahabuleshwar, in the Western Ghaut mountains, now the summer residence of the Bombay Government and its officers. No finer historical site than this is to be found in all India. The rock-citadel stands up majestically against the sky. From there Sivaji issued forth with a single attendant to meet the Moslem envoy on a trysting spot at its base — the Moslem cavalry being posted at a little distance off in an open space surrounded by dense thicket. As the two chiefs met and embraced, Sivaji, whose hands were secretly armed with steel claws like those of a tiger, inflicted deadly wounds on the envoy. A signal gun from the citadel announced that the deed had been done. Thereon a destructive fire was poured upon the Moslem cavalry from the thicket, which was alive with Mahratta musketeers. A Moslem tomb still remains to mark the spot where the envoy fell ; and therefrom, as the situation is an elevated one, the shimmering ocean may be descried in the background. Here then is a clear landmark in the modern history of India.

It may be hard to connect the early stages in the rise of the British power with known localities. The garden at Plassey can scarcely be made out, where Clive paced up and down revolving the question whether he should give battle against overwhelming numbers, and fight one of the decisive contests in the history of the nations. Probably the positions could not be marked out, at least with any impressive effect, of the battle at Buxar which gave us the command of the mid-Gangetic valley, or of Lord Lake's victories which made us masters of Delhi and the surrounding provinces, hardly even of Assaye where Arthur Wellesley struck a fatal blow at the Mahratta power. But the positions of Arcot, Vellore, and Trichinopoly may be examined, and they are all striking to the eye—abrupt rock-masses fortified, and rising out of cultivated and irrigated plains. Here by divers actions was fought out the warlike controversy between the English and French regarding the possession of southern or peninsular India. Here, too, no generous Englishman can fail to appreciate the genius of our French rival Dupleix.

Parallel with the British in Western India, the Portuguese established a commerce and a dominion which for some few generations flourished splendidly, and then decayed rapidly. The ruins of old Goa (as distinguished from the new), the remains of the cathedral and the palaces, now half hidden by jungly overgrowth, the tomb and shrine of the great missionary St. Xavier, are interesting though melancholy. The ruins of Bassein—once a place of equal status with Bombay—

with the walls standing of churches, and of stately residences on the lines of the desolate streets—afford a peculiarly weird spectacle by moonlight.

At Seringapatam amidst the Mysore mountains—where the streets are still standing in what is almost a city of death—may be distinctly seen the camp of the besieging British, the ridge of their breaching batteries, the line of their storming, and the breach where the defender Tippoo Sultan died fighting. This decisive event, near the close of the eighteenth century, assured to us the supremacy of South-Western India.

At Poona we see a fine artificial lake, in the midst of which there rises a large fortified rock, crowned with Hindu temples. On the highest terrace in one of these temples sat the last of the Mahratta Peshwas, watching in despair the conflict he had madly provoked between his own forces and the British troops at Kirki on the undulating plain near Poona. This was another of those decisive days, during the early part of the

LAKE AT POONA

nineteenth century, in the formation of the British Empire. The Maharatta confederacy was ended, though some of its members still survived under British suzerainty. The British position in Western India was secured, with a broad territory called the British Deccan in contradistinction to the old Native Deccan.

The succeeding generation was remarkable for consolidation rather than for conquest and extension. But, near the middle of the century, five crucial battles were fought with the Sikhs in two wars, the most strenuous ever waged by the British Government with Indian races. On the left bank of the Sutlej may be observed quite exactly the grounds where the fights raged at Moodki, at Ferozshah, and at Sobraon in the first war. The *terrain* is not striking to the eye in any one of these three battle scenes. Still the visitor, as he rides over the undulating plains, now richly cultivated, close to the great river, cannot but reflect on the gravity of the results from these victories almost snatched from fate by British valour and endurance, and on the coincidence that hereabouts was the invasion of Alexander stayed and his boundary pillars erected. In the second war, however, the battlefield of Chillianwala is picturesquely marked. It lies close to that low jungle which was very embarrassing to the British during the fight. Around it are the low hills overlooking the Jhelum River, on the banks of which Alexander defeated King Porus (already mentioned in the last Chapter), and so seized the control of North-Western India. At some little distance from these hills was won the crowning victory of Goojerat; but the fight was on an even plain, now cultivated; the limits of the battlefield are precisely known, but nothing further is to be seen.

The scenes of the actions whereby the British Government retrieved the disasters of the Mutinies in 1857 are indeed many; but generally it is difficult to denote the localities. Nevertheless, the scenes at Delhi can be clearly perceived: the balcony overlooking the Jamna, where the feeble descendant of the Great Mogul stood to accept from the mutinous native cavalry-troopers standing beneath him, the offer of an Imperial status ; the tree in the palace courtyard where the European prisoners were murdered with his sanction ; the ridge outside the city where the British besieging force held its own for months ; the Cashmere Gate, still thickly sprinkled with marks from cannon-shot, where the assault was delivered ; the several points where the city was recaptured ; the neighbouring shrine where the *soi-disant* Emperor was made prisoner. The events in the relief and final recapture of Lucknow cannot, perhaps, be so exactly followed on the spot ; still, the Bailey Guard and the Residency remain in some degree, to preserve the memory of one of the most heroic defences in British annals. The well at Cawnpore, containing the remains of the murdered Europeans, is marked by a white marble monument of touching beauty, and surrounded by a rose-garden.

The wars in Burma could hardly be recalled to memory by localities admitting of examination. But at Rangoon, on the estuary of the Irawady, the terraced and fortified pagodas may be seen which were stormed by the British troops.

Afghanistan does not fall within the range of this work, although it has been closely connected with the history of India. Otherwise it would be a pleasure to describe the localities—in and about Caubul, on the road to Jelalabad, at the Ghuzni fortress, on the road to Candahar, at Candahar itself, and in the regions near it—where British valour even to death has been displayed, sometimes in disaster, but more often in victory.

In respect to the recent military events on the North-Western Frontier, the hillside of Dargai, and several points on the road to Chitral will be marked for the consideration of those who may come after.

APPENDIX

SOME LEADING STATISTICS.

AREA.

	ENGLISH SQ. MILES.
Empire of India	1,560,160
Of which the British Territories have	964,993
And the Native States	595,167

POPULATION.

	SOULS.
Empire of India (Census of 1891)	287,123,350
Of which British Territories have	221,172,952
And Native States	65,950,398

In the British Territories—

Bengal has	71,346,987
Bombay Presidency	18,901,123
Madras	35,630,440

APPENDIX

PRINCIPAL TOWNS.

	POPULATION.
Calcutta, with Suburbs	861,764
Madras	452,518
Bombay	821,764
Hyderabad (Deccan)	415,039
Delhi	192,579
Poona	161,390
Peshawar	84,191

RELIGIONS, EMPIRE OF INDIA.

(Census of 1891.)

	POPULATION.
Hindu	207,731,727
Sikh	1,907,838
Jain	1,416,638
Booddhist	7,131,361
Parsi	89,904
Muhammadans	57,321,164
Christians	2,284,380

ARMY.

	OFFICERS AND MEN.
European	74,299
Native	140,640
Total	214,939

APPENDIX

REVENUES, &c.

	TENS OF RUPEES X.
Revenues and Receipts (annual) . .	98,370,167
Public Debt	232,389,028

EXTERNAL TRADE:

Imports (Annual).

Merchandise	76,103,948
Treasure	13,084,563

Exports.

Merchandise	103,984,096
Treasure	4,937,495
Grand Total . .	198,110,103

RAILWAYS.

Miles open (1897)	20,390

EDUCATION.

Colleges and Schools	152,841
Scholars	4,303,109

APPENDIX

POST OFFICE (1896).

Post-offices and Letter-boxes	25,515
Letters, newspapers, &c., carried	423,925,276

ELECTRIC TELEGRAPH.

Miles of wire	142,926
„ line	46,375
Number of paid messages	4,736,734

AGRICULTURE.

Population employed in	171,735,000

FORESTS.

	SQ. MILES.
Reserved by the State	76,400

MILLS.

Cotton	147
Jute	28
Woollen	6
Paper	8

	TENS OF RS. X.
Total capital paid up of mills and presses	13,687,799

APPENDIX

GOVERNORS-GENERAL AND VICEROYS,

WITH DATES OF THEIR ASSUMPTION OF OFFICE.

Warren Hastings	1774
Earl Cornwallis	1786
Lord Teignmouth	1793
Marquis Wellesley	1798
Marquis Cornwallis	1805
Earl of Minto	1807
Earl of Moira (Marquis of Hastings)	1813
Earl Amherst	1823
Lord William Bentinck	1828
Earl of Auckland	1836
Earl of Ellenborough	1842
Sir Henry (Lord) Hardinge	1844
Earl (Marquis) of Dalhousie	1848
Earl Canning	1856
Earl of Elgin	1862
Sir John (Lord) Lawrence	1864
Earl of Mayo	1869
Lord (Earl of) Northbrook	1872
Lord (Earl) Lytton	1876
Marquis of Ripon	1880
Earl (Marquis) of Dufferin	1884
Marquis of Lansdowne	1888
Earl of Elgin	1894

PRINCIPAL DATES OF INDIAN HISTORY.

The Vedas, supposed date	B.C. 1500
The "Mahabharat," supposed date	1300

APPENDIX

"Rama and the Ramayana," supposed date	B.C.	1200
The Code of Manu	,, .	700
Brahmanism	,, .	600
The Booddhist Reformation	,, .	500
Invasion by Alexander the Great	,, .	327
Chandra Goopta	,, .	300
Emperor Asoka, Booddhist	,, .	230
"Vikramaditya"	,, . A.D.	500
Restoration of Brahmanism		550
First Moslem Invasion		1001
First Charter of East India Company		1600
Mogul Empire under Akber the Great		1605
Mahratta Insurrection under Sivaji		1657
Death of Mogul Emperor Aurangzebe		1707
Battle of Plassey (Clive)		1757
Defeat of the Mahrattas by Moslems		1761
Fall of Seringapatam		1799
Final Defeat of Mahrattas by British		1818
First Afghan War		1838
Annexation of the Panjab		1849
Outbreak of the Mutinies		1857
East India Company's rule gives place to the direct administration of the British Crown		1858
Queen Victoria proclaimed Empress of India		1877